WITHDRAWN

VALUES, LEADERSHIP AND QUALITY:

The Administration of Higher Education

David Dodds Henry

President, University of Illinois
1955-71

The David D. Henry Lectures
1979-85

VALUES, LEADERSHIP AND QUALITY:
The Administration of Higher Education

With an Introduction by
Stanley O. Ikenberry
President, University of Illinois

Distributed by the University of Illinois Press

© Copyright 1990 by the Board of Trustees of the University of Illinois

Library of Congress Catalog Card No.: 90-70935

Contents

Introduction 1
    STANLEY O. IKENBERRY

Biography of David Dodds Henry............................ 5

Quality and Equality in
Health Professions Education and Service...................... 8
    LLOYD C. ELAM

How We Talk and How We Act:
Administrative Theory and
Administrative Life... 36
    JAMES G. MARCH

The Liberal Arts Revisited
    HANNA HOLBORN GRAY................................... 82

The University Presidency:
Comparative Reflections on Leadership........................ 94
    MARTIN A. TROW

Innovation and Tradition
in Higher Education..146
    JOHN B. SLAUGHTER

Introduction

The five lectures contained in this book were delivered as part of a lecture series named in honor of former University of Illinois President David Dodds Henry. At the conclusion of his distinguished sixteen-year presidency (1955-1971), the Board of Trustees of the University of Illinois established the David D. Henry Lecture series to honor the man and to further the profession to which his life has been dedicated. The Henry Lectures are endowed through gifts to the University of Illinois Foundation. Sites of the Henry Lectures rotate between the Urbana and Chicago campuses of the University of Illinois.

The common theme of the lectures revolves around broadly defined issues related to the administration of higher education. It was Dr. Henry's belief that this subject had received too little attention from those who would improve our education system. "Within the area of knowledge about higher education," he wrote in 1971, "the least understood component is administration. I regard the administration of higher education as a specialty whose study is as exacting in knowledge as medicine, as central to effective operation as law, as sensitive to human relations as government. The study is that of an art and science, and constitutes a discipline in its own right."

It is fitting that a forum for discussion of excellence in higher education be named in honor of David Dodds Henry. His sixteen years at the helm of the University of Illinois were marked by extraordinary growth, change and improvements. Under his guidance, the University established a new Chicago campus, expanded the health sciences program, enlarged its libraries and generally strengthened its role as a world-class institution. Dr. Henry remained a national spokesman for higher education long past his two university presidencies. His leadership greatly inflenced national organizations such as the American Council on Education, the Carnegie Foundation for the Advancement of Teaching and the National Association of State Universities and Land-Grant Colleges. In short, all of us involved in the administration of higher education owe David Henry a debt of gratitude for his many contributions and thoughtful leadership.

The subjects addressed in this volume are as diverse as the speakers who delivered them, yet they all pose questions that are central to the mission of higher education. And those questions are no less pertinent today than when the Henry lecturers posed them. What should an educated person know? How can we ensure equal access to higher education? How can university leaders balance their symbolic, political and managerial roles? How does the changing face of our student body affect the way we teach and the courses we offer? And how do we synthesize the new partnerships between private industry and universities with the public mandates of higher education? Lloyd Elam, James March, Hanna Gray, Martin Trow and John Slaughter tackle these and other relevant questions with thoughtful skill.

Dr. Lloyd Elam, president of Meharry Medical College when he delivered the 1979 lecture, argues that quality and equality in the education of health care professionals and in the delivery of health care services are inextricably linked. Equality in medical school admission policies, he said — prophetically, it turns out — is expressed through reduced emphasis on memorization of fact and increased attention to the character and commitment of the applicant. He further suggests that measurements of quality in the delivery of health care services must take into account the accessibility of those services to all segments of our society.

Dr. James March of Stanford University offers the opinion that successful leaders in higher education recognize the importance of routine processes, those activities that keep institutions running. Making a big and complex university work, he says, involves "the execution of large numbers of small things." And, contrary to conventional wisdom, Dr. March suggests that universities are not rigid institutions: They simply do not change in ways that totally satisfy any one group or interest.

President Hanna Holborn Gray of the University or Chicago delivers an eloquent defense of the liberal arts in her address. Accepting the notion that the liberal arts are "those studies worthy of a free man," she goes on to define freedom as "a state of informed cultural awareness and capacity for critical judgment." Dr. Gray holds the view that the value of liberal arts education be judged neither in terms of narrow vocationalism, nor as a core curriculum to address the specific dilemmas of social living, but rather in terms of its contribution to overall intellectual competence.

Professor Martin Trow of the University of California at Berkeley describes higher education leadership as having symbolic, political, managerial and academic components. The university president, he believes, has the ability to project the characters and values of an institution. At the same time, he or she must possess the ability to resolve the conflicting demands and pressures of many internal and external constituencies.

University students should have a greater appreciation for "both Milton and molecules, both Carlyle and chemistry," says John Slaughter, chancellor of the University of Maryland when he delivered the 1985 Henry Lecture. Dr. Slaughter suggests that the liberal arts are important not just because they make better professionals, but because they teach civic responsibility. It is the job of university administrators, he suggests, to help their graduate schools strike a more equitable balance between research and the basic "core curricula" of the liberal arts. To that task he adds recruitment of minority students as two of the most important issues facing leaders of higher education.

The first five Henry Lectures (1972-1978) are contained in a volume titled *Conflict, Retrenchment, and Reappraisal: The Administration of Higher Education.* This book contains the second five lectures, delivered from 1979-1985. Each lecture is followed by a text of the discussion that followed the speaker's address. It is our hope that readers will draw insight and inspiration from the wisdom shared in these pages, and that the lecture series that bears his name will continue to honor the many contributions of David Dodds Henry.

Stanley O. Ikenberry
President, University of Illinois

Biography
of David D. Henry

As president of the University of Illinois, David D. Henry headed a system of educationally autonomous campuses, two in Chicago (at the Medical Center and at Chicago Circle) and the oldest in Urbana-Champaign, with a combined enrollment of 60,000 in 1971.

Dr. Henry was appointed as the twelfth president of the University of Illinois in 1955 and retired in 1971. From 1952 to 1955 he was executive vice-chancellor of New York University and from 1945 to 1952 president of Wayne University, Detroit.

Dr. Henry's early professional experience included service as instructor in a land-grant college, as teacher and department head in a small liberal arts college, and as deputy for higher education in a state department of higher education, leading to his service as chief executive officer and later president of a large municipal university and chief educational officer for the nation's largest independent university.

Dr. Henry has also served higher education in many important as-assignments. He is one of the few to have headed six of the most influential national organizations dealing with college and university affairs. He served as chairman of the American Council on Education and of the Carnegie Foundation for the Advancement of Teaching, and as president of the Association of Urban Universities, of the National Commission on Accrediting, of the National Association of State Universities and Land-Grant Colleges, and of the Association of American Universities.

In addition to giving leadership to organizations in higher education, Dr. Henry served on several national study groups: the Carnegie Commission on Educational Television, the President's Committee on Education beyond the High School (vice-chairman), the Carnegie Commission on Higher Education, and the National Board on Graduate Education (chairman).

Dr. Henry has written and spoken widely on educational subjects. His bibliography includes four books and over 300 contributions to professional journals, periodicals, and collections.

Dr. Henry became president emeritus of the University of Illinois on September 1, 1971. He was then appointed distinguished professor of higher education in the College of Education of the University at Urbana-Champaign, becoming professor emeritus in 1974.

Born in Pennsylvania October 21, 1905, Dr. Henry received three degrees from Pennsylvania State University — an A.B. in 1926, an A.M. in 1927, and a Ph.D. in 1931. He holds honorary degrees from twenty-nine institutions and membership in thirteen honor societies.

Lloyd C. Elam, M.D., is an authority on the study and practice of psychiatric medicine and an enduring leader at Meharry Medical College, where he served as president from 1968-1981. Dr. Elam received his medical degree from the University of Washington–Seattle in 1957. He performed his internship at the University of Illinois Hospital in Chicago, from 1957 to 1958, and was in residency at the University of Chicago Department of Psychiatry from 1958 to 1961. He established the Department of Psychiatry at Hubbard Hospital at Meharry Medical College, and continues to serve on its staff as a distinguished service professor.

Dr. Elam is a member of more than thirty professional, educational, social, religious civic, business and governmental organizations. They include the American Medical Association, the American Psychiatric Association and the R. F. Boyd Medical Society. He is on the board of directors of The Alfred P. Sloan Foundation, and the Board of Health and the Department of Mental Health in Tennessee. He has received many honors and awards, including three honorary doctoral degrees, for his administrative and moral leadership on behalf of better health and education for all of our citizens.

The sixth Henry Lecture was presented April 11, 1979, at the University of Illinois Medical Center in Chicago.

Quality and Equality
in Health Professions Education and Service

by Lloyd C. Elam, M.D.
President, Meharry Medical College

Thank you very much, Dr. Begando, for those nice words. Dr. Henry, it is a delight to see you and to be a part of this program established in your name. For anyone who has received some part of his or her education at the University of Illinois, there can surely be few greater honors than to be invited back as a Henry Lecturer. In returning after twenty years I am impressed by the changes I see, not only in physical appearance of the Medical Center but also in terms of where this campus is going.

Earlier lecturers in this series have addressed some of the major concerns and thrusts of higher education in general. Today I wish to consider a dimension of comparable significance, the issue of quality and equality in health professions education and service. In doing so I will underscore my observation that the University of Illinois is one of a few places in the country where a minority person would be invited to talk about quality. Generally, when University communities think about minorities there is accompanying anxiety about maintaining quality. As a matter of fact, one of the reasons for widespread concern about the present thrust to increase the number of minority persons in upper-division programs is a fear that educational quality will be diminished. You will understand, then, why I am particularly proud that the institution of which I am an alumnus would invite one of my race to talk about quality, as well as equality, in health professions education and service.

As background let me say that we are very fortunate to live at the zenith of development of medical science and health services based on that science. Never before have so many people been involved in providing health care to others: 426,000 physicians; 122,000 dentists; 961,000 nurses; 4,393,000 other professionals. A total of 5,902,000 individuals are involved in delivering health services.

And never before has health care been so effective. Diseases which were scourges only a decade ago are now controllable or extinct. In the United States, for example, smallpox and diphtheria are museum relics; malaria is only known because of world travel; and poliomyelitis and measles could join the others if we chose. Not only the infectious diseases but all of the major killers of mankind are on the decrease in the United States except cancer, suicide, and accidents. In the field of mental health, manic depressive illness, which affected some of the most successful persons with periods of incapacity, can now be controlled, and many other mental diseases, like the phobias, are curable by new psychological approaches. The success of therapies in the mental health field must certainly be approaching that which has been achieved with infectious diseases. Problems of diagnosis have been equally susceptible to solution through new laboratory aids and such technical advances as the CAT scanner.

Never before have so many sectors of the economy been involved in expanding the armamentarium against sickness. A single pharmaceutical house will spend as much as $300 million for research in a single year, and the investments by all segments of government in research and service are among the most useful expenditures of tax money.

And yet never before have so many taken it upon themselves to criticize the health care in this country. An informed example of that criticism is *The Quality of Mercy* by Selig Greenborg, who gives what he calls "A Report on the Critical Condition of Hospital and Medical Care in America." He applauds the teaching hospital for all it can do and the efforts of the staff to meet each person's needs. But he is a critic and suggests areas which require serious attention in every aspect of the system. Says Greenborg:

> While medical research unquestionably deserves continued massive support, correction of the lopsided imbalance between it and the financing of services, along with the training of many more people to apply knowledge, is long overdue.
>
> ...The greatest need today in the world's richest nation is not for organ transplants or for some of the other marvels of the latest medical technology, but for wider availability of the now commonplace results of the research of twenty-five or even fifty years ago.

And yet the perceived need to make major changes in the system is not just a reflection of the desire of the intellect to always do better — it is rather a recognition that a certain kind of synthesis is necessary.

For more than 100 years there has been a relentless effort to improve health professions education. During that time there have been such tremendous breakthroughs in our knowledge of preventive and curative medicine that *quality* medical care now has real meaning in terms of outcome — in terms of what can be done to prolong life and diminish suffering.

In other sectors of society, and with the same relentlessness, the struggle for *equality* has also brought about gradual but significant change. Although equality is a generally understood term it may mean different things to different people. In education, it usually implies equal opportunity. In health care it suggests equal access to all services. For the politically minded it means representation based on percent of the population. For the health worker it means pay based on the job performed. Since equality has all these meanings, the health system must accommodate itself to all of them or be accused of fostering inequality.

Initially the problem was resistance to the concept of equality as appropriate for the health field. More recently this view was replaced by a scarcity philosophy, in which it was assumed that there were not enough health care jobs to go around and thus it was justified to award the available places to an elite. However, whether health care is considered a right or a necessity, equity would demand withholding some care from *all* if the premise is accepted that there will not be enough to go around. Since this is unacceptable to both consumers and providers, because it reduces the quality of health service, current thrusts have attempted to move health care out of the economy of scarcity. These efforts are manifested by the increasing numbers being educated as health professionals, the increasing variety of health professions, and the drive to provide additional services in areas that have been underserved. Although health planners sometimes consider scarcity a necessary means of controlling the escalation of costs, a more logical system is surely needed.

What I am saying is that for more than a century many individuals have worked diligently to improve *quality* in health professions education and health service, and during the same period others have worked to improve *equality* of opportunity and of access to those same things. The difficulties begin when you try to combine the two. It is the kind of trouble an administrator encounters when trying to implement equal opportunity programs in education or to provide services which assure not only equal access but also payment of providers on the basis of the service they perform rather than the label they wear. You can surely picture the controversy that would accompany paying the nurse what a doctor is paid for doing the same thing. Nobody wants to argue against the merits of improved quality or extension of equality. It is only when we attempt a synthesis of the two that a solution for one seems to confound the other. We need to ask ourselves whether this is an inevitability or the result of missed opportunities in the past.

The present generation of health professions educators faces a fierce attack on all those ingredients that have traditionally been designed to guarantee quality in education and practice. Today the patterns of the past are being challenged in many ways. Among the most significant may be the diminishing financial resources at a time of increasing costs. For example, during fiscal year 1979 federal guidelines seek to hold the annual increase of hospital costs to 9 percent when inflation, the increase in the cost of energy, and wage increases in general will predictably exceed that amount. Secondly, there is a growing sophistication of the populace with a resulting increase in demand for more, as well as more elaborate, health services for all the people. Further, the profession is faced with steady advances in medical knowledge and expertise, which together increase the educational and service options at a time when there is also growing pressure to accept a more heterogeneous student body.

The system is being shaken by a growing demand to establish collegial patterns of institutional governance along with mounting insistence upon community participation in decision making. Although collegial patterns of governance have always been a part of the University scene, only recently have medical, dental, nursing, pharmacy, and other health professions faculties exhibited great concern for those matters. In the past deans, presidents, and other administrative officers have often functioned in faculty roles as well, and there was little difficulty in perceiving such individuals as wearing two hats simultaneously. However, as faculties are unionized, as community pressures on universities mount, and as accountability becomes more common as a tool for external control, health science faculties demand greater participation in institutional management. Finally, institutions must respond to the rising expectation that they will produce graduates who will gravitate to less desirable parts of the country to live and to practice. The maldistribution of health professionals and health services continues to be among the greatest failures of the health system in every country in the world. All of these new emphases raise the question of whether today's educators can develop the pattern of health professions education which will serve this evolving health system.

The definition of quality in health professions education is not as critical as its recognition. In a very enjoyable discussion in *Zen and the Art of Motorcycle Maintenance,* the point is made that when quality exists it is recognizable whether we are observing a painting, listening to music, or repairing a machine. Similarly, in health services it is not the definition of high quality care which is the goal (for somehow when it is present we can recognize it), but rather assuring the delivery of high quality service should be the objective. Although some people have tried to quantitate quality, in the absence of certainty about what constitutes quality substitutes are frequently employed — popularity, opulence, being the only one in town, being the largest in town, or being better than the others in some measurable dimension may be chosen as goals. All of these have been utilized in varying degrees and at times are even quantified to suggest that they are approximations of the real thing. However, these substitutes cannot be allowed to eclipse what is basic and fundamental.

To assure the achievement of quality in health professions education we have relied first on the selection of the most successful students for admission to these programs, since past success is among the best predictors of future success. Historically many factors have been used to identify these "successful" candidates: those from the most successful families, the offspring of successful alumni, those with the highest scores or grades in college, those who were most like the selectors. These have all been used to choose who will be admitted to health professions schools. All have varying degrees of credibility. Although these may be simplistic ways of promoting quality, no better ways have been found to date. But I want to make it very clear that I refer to choosing those who will be most *successful*, not simply those who have the most of some particular thing. We all will recognize the scriptural principle "To him who hath it shall be given." However, if we only admit to medicine those who have the most, whether it is money, scores, experiences, or family background, we cannot effectively address the question of equality. To deal with both quality *and* equality, we must choose the most successful, not just those who have the most of any one of these elements. Educators who, in this day of rising concern for human rights and insistence upon affirmative action, fear that quality will suffer can be reassured. Choosing the most successful persons from other races, other communities, or the other gender will all contribute to insuring quality, since people successful in many dimensions are more likely to be successful health educators and health providers.

The second ingredient in contributing to quality is knowledge. There is no question in any educator's mind about the necessity to have a fund of knowledge which is constantly being reviewed and updated if graduates are to practice modern health care. Because of the requirement for knowledge, numerous organizations have been developed to assure the public that this base is present: testing organizations such as the National Board of Medical Examiners, or the National League for Nursing, or the specialty boards in other health professions. One of the consequences of this reliance on knowledge is an increase in specialization. By becoming a specialist, health professionals can cope with the increasing amounts of knowledge required for effective practice by reducing the scope of the data which must be mastered. This also increases the time available to keep abreast of new developments in the field.

The emphasis on knowledge as an index of quality has also elevated the importance of memorization. Thus high rewards are given to students who memorize easily, in the belief that they will have learned what is necessary to be a good practitioner. When they do well on evaluative tests, teachers also feel successful. It is therefore understandable that faculty members may feel that quality is threatened when the need for equality of opportunity forces acceptance of students who have not perfected a talent for rote memory and are slower at data recall.

In addition, the need for more doctors for family medicine causes concern in the face of the vast amount of knowledge to be mastered, or memorized, in order to understand complex scientific principles. Fortunately the new emphasis on problem solving and the use of problem-oriented records are examples of attempts to reduce rote memory as the principal means of learning. It is generally acknowledged that the use of information in problem solving is a natural method of learning, one far superior to simple memorization of a large number of facts. Quality and equality will both be better served by these new advances in medical education and in health care.

The third ingredient which has historically been used to promote quality is insistence upon standards, and the employment of varied techniques to monitor how well these standards are met. The existence of such organizations as the American Medical Association, the American Nursing Association, the American Hospital Association, the State Licensing Boards, the American Boards of Medical Specialties, and the Professional Standards Review Organizations is an example of the system designed to keep standards high and to provide reasonable assurance that those standards are met. The ease with which standards can be established by governmental bodies is such that some think that setting standards is the major method of insuring quality. This may be all that governments *can* do, but a problem is introduced when the purpose of these mechanisms is diverted to achieve other goals. For example, for many years membership in a county medical society of the AMA was necessary to obtain staff privileges in many hospitals. This was designed to assure high quality health service, but when it was also used as a method to enforce racial discrimination equality in health care delivery suffered. Similarly, the Professional Standards

Review Organizations was initially designed to maintain quality, but when it was misused to control costs the basic purpose was compromised and health care suffered.

The basic functions served by all of these organizations are necessary. As health care is broadened, a wider variety of diagnostic and therapeutic options will become available. In addition to doctors' offices, clinics, and hospitals, an array of neighborhood health centers, new types of surgery centers, special purpose single organ centers (like renal disease centers), and primary care centers staffed by special professionals (like nurse practitioners) will all become more prominent. Instead of using the traditional indirect measures of quality (comparing such variables as manpower, budget, patient flow, facilities, etc., among institutions), direct measures (like outcome) will need to be used, for a better outcome is the real goal of health care. The fact that the input includes more practitioners or a different array or those who have different training is irrelevant if outcome is the measure of quality. Outcome standards will not only permit a broader selection of manpower for quality health service but will contribute to the achievement of equality as well.

A fourth key element in the search for quality is the judicious use of rewards. Two major reward systems are those which are external to the individual (like salary increments or faculty rank) and those which are internal (like the satisfaction which comes from having done a job well). Overemphasis on the external reward system causes many to forget that which comes from within. At the present time great attention is given to external rewards because of the materialistic orientation of our society and because they provide a tool for manipulating health care providers. External reward systems have been entirely adequate in the past to reinforce the search for quality. But, as we seek to expand the health care system, the external reward system (especially money) impedes rather than aids the effort to broaden the distribution of quality. The most flagrant example of this is relating Medicare payments to the "usual and customary fee." This encourages practice in the "overdoctored" areas (where fees are customarily higher) and penalizes those who practice in rural areas or among the poor. The internal rewards associated with fulfilling an important social and professional purpose may be displaced by those that are merely monetary.

A fifth ingredient of quality assurance in a technological culture is the presence of an adequate number and variety of facilities and modern equipment. However, the belief of some health planners that the easiest way to cut costs is to limit the amount of sophisticated equipment in certain areas does not take into account the additive quality produced by much of the new hardware. The extension of high quality health care to those who have not had it demands that the benefits of each technologic advance be made available to the newly-to-be-served population, not only to those who already have the most.

The sixth ingredient of quality assurance is the organization of a system for providing adequate care. This involves highly qualified physicians, a complement of sensitive and dedicated support personnel, ready availability of necessary drugs, and an internal monitoring structure that can determine both the degree to which quality goals are reached and future needs and directions. Of course this component is not always appreciated by the target groups whose cultural orientation is toward a day-to-day satisfaction of needs and who seek only episodic care. At the other extreme are those providers interested in only one segment of the health service complex (like the proprietary hospital) and who often fail to appreciate the entire system. Health maintenance organizations, for example, are reputedly concerned with aspects of the system which can be organized to provide better care, care at less cost, and/or care to a broader population.

I would like now to turn your attention from quality to equality — the most elusive of our goals. What is equality in the field of health professions education and health services? Is it equal access to medical care when it is needed? Is it the provision of educational opportunities for the most successful blacks, Chicanos, or women? Looking at equality historically, we must acknowledge that there has never been a serious attempt within the health field to objectively define it in either education or care. As an outgrowth of the civil rights movement of the 1960s, a project sponsored by the Association of American Medical Colleges, the National Medical Fellowship, the National Medical Association, and the Macy Foundation, among others, aimed to increase minority representation in medical classes to 10 percent, with the assumption that this would correct the serious shortage of blacks and other minorities in the medical field. Although many said, "It cannot be done," the tremendous progress made within five years raised the proportion of minorities from 2 percent to 7 percent of the entering class. The absolute number was even more impressive, since size of medical classes grew steadily larger during that period.

Despite such initial success it was then claimed that this achievement merely reflected the large pool of applicants who had been denied admission in the past but would not continue as the backlog was absorbed. Contrary to this belief, even as money for special recruitment has decreased, there has been only a small reduction in the number of interested minorities and no evidence that those applying are less qualified, according to college grades or MCAT scores, than those in the earlier pool. It was finally argued that the efforts to increase minority representation were unfair, certainly too expensive, and might be illegal. Following the Bakke decision at least a few schools reduced their special efforts to recruit minorities.

The background for this pessimism is sordid. During the early years in this country, there was a general belief that blacks did not possess the intelligence required to learn medicine. As a matter of fact, the first black person to receive a medical degree in America was sent to school on a wager that he could not succeed. After he graduated, it was decided in some states that blacks should not become doctors, for those who did would have too much mobility and might foment insurrection against the slave practices. In many states, including my present one, laws were passed prohibiting blacks from practicing medicine. These laws were abolished after the Civil War, and since then there has been no prohibition against blacks being educated in medicine. For many years over three-fourths were educated in two predominantly black medical schools, Howard and Meharry, but until the 1950s those graduates were barred from membership in most medical societies and from practicing in many hospitals. The black doctor, excluded from many medical schools, medical societies, and hospitals was denied not only the opportunity for personal growth but also was forced to fight for both equality and quality if black people were to benefit from the advances in medicine.

Some of these inequalities existed for other minorities as well. The medical profession, which has led other professions in its search for quality, had to be (and still is to some degree) dragged screaming and kicking by the civil rights and human rights movements into activity designed to promote equality. But progress was made. In 1968 when I left Chicago there were only nineteen black students in all the medical schools in the city. By 1975 the University of Illinois alone admitted that many and in subsequent years exceeded that number. I would like to offer my special commendation to the University for that outstanding effort. While the number of black student applicants has leveled off, or shown a small decrease since 1975, and there has been a decrease in the number accepted as well, there has at the same time been less pressure to provide equality of educational opportunity. What will happen when that pressure disappears?

One other change which deserves note is the changing role of the historically black medical institutions. Two questions have had to be faced: (1) Does the existence of these schools promote equality or inequality? (2) If they are to exist, how can they best contribute to improving the quality of education and service? Meharry Medical College in Nashville, Tennessee, set about to address both these challenges. The finding of the courts could not be refuted — to have segregated schools, whether black or white, whether in lower or higher education, meant unequal schools. Most particularly, the financial support was not equal, and this affected everything else. How then could the school make a contribution to equality? Of course exclusion of nonblacks had to stop immediately, just as exclusion of blacks had to cease in other schools. This alone was not enough. The next step was to define an area of concern which would provide an institutional focus — one in which this school had advantages — and concentrate on it. This is not a new approach since it is the basis of specialization and division of labor which together have contributed so greatly to quality and production. The school chose as its focus comprehensive ambulatory health care. This was both compatible and consistent with its traditional role of concern for the disadvantaged and with existing interests in the community. The subsequent popularity of primary care and the need for all institutions to address the most pressing needs in medical education with limited resources simply contributed to the momentum.

The next step was to study the options for ambulatory health care and to determine the most effective one. The alternatives we studied were the neighborhood health center model; the hospital-based ambulatory care center model; and traditional approaches using doctors' offices, emergency rooms, and outpatient clinics. A seven-year longitudinal study indicated that there was no significant difference in the outcome of the overall health of a community served by a neighborhood health center and one served by the hospital-based center, but that the presence of some kind of organized program was superior to none, especially for such areas as prenatal care and the discovery time for new diseases.

Concurrently, research was undertaken in the educational area to determine what measurable criteria could predict, with greater accuracy than MCAT scores and GPAs alone, which applicants would be successful in medical school and which would need special assistance. The curriculum was also altered to provide several tracks, some of which were optional, but all of which were selected on the basis of preliminary data from the predictor study. This investigation is continuing, and the predictors are not yet sufficiently firm for publication. I can say that they are based on data obtained from the MCAT science section, the UP-Biology test (Educational Testing Service), the AAMC Biochemistry Placement Test (1975), the Nelson-Denny Reading Score — Form C, and performance in a concentrated three-week cell biology course at Meharry.

While National Board examinations, and similar testing procedures, are obviously useful for end-of-year or end-of-semester student assessment, systematic use of problem-oriented medical records is an ideal method for providing feedback on students' day-to-day data collection, diagnostic, and problem-solving skills. Both tools are useful in self-pacing as well as in choosing the proper educational track. And some degree of self-pacing is absolutely essential when students with greatly differing backgrounds, abilities, and interests are members of the same class. These two advances in medical education planning and implementation have been far more effective in facilitating student achievement than any of the curriculum time and course manipulations that have been more popular.

At the same time, in order to fulfill this important focus, the institution decided that it should get involved in similar efforts in some developing countries. One of the most rewarding things we did was to go to Botswana and retrain all the nurses in that country to become providers of primary health care. Shortly thereafter Norway provided the assistance required to build clinics throughout that land. Today every citizen of Botswana is within walking distance of a clinic staffed by a trained nurse practitioner. This has been a remarkable experience from which we learned many things, for example, the usefulness of having mothers keep each child's health record. Thus, wherever the mother goes she can provide for the nurse practitioner or physician an accurate account of the child's past history and management, and that practitioner can then add the current symptoms, findings, and treatment. The record is always current and is always available wherever the mother may take her child.

This background information on the search for quality in education and service by the health professions in general, the recent moves toward equality in both spheres, and the work at one predominantly black medical college lead me to the following conclusions and recommendations:

1. Equality and quality can go hand in hand, but they do not do so automatically. It is easier and less expensive to provide high quality for the few. Segregation has been the traditional way of solving problems in order to save money. However, it leads to a two-class health care system. With such an approach, the number included in the first class steadily diminishes as more and more of them begin to get second-class education and health care. Only by insisting on equality will we be forced to correct the weakness of the present system — a weakness that exists because decisions are made for the benefit of the providers on the assumption that some consumers can be ignored.

2. The persons who should become health care providers must be chosen from the most successful individuals from a wide variety of

backgrounds. Being the most successful includes making acceptable grades in college and scores on tests, but many other factors must also be considered. For example, the most successful applicant from rural USA may have a lower MCAT score than the most successful applicant from the suburbs. Both have a place in medicine in order to justify the goal of equality and to provide care to the two different localities.

3. The school must be able to predict success and failure with a great degree of accuracy and to provide individual feedback all along the educational continuum. The frequent failure of health professions schools to do so reflects an attitude inherited from the graduate education model, in which the responsibility for learning is on the students. In the professional schools this responsibility must be shared by the institution. Recent advances in teaching techniques enhance the ability to ensure high quality graduates even with a more diverse student body than was present in the past.

4. Learning by use (which is far superior to present reliance on memorization and testing) is underemphasized because it requires more of teachers. Problem solving, rather than the acquisition of facts alone, should become the mode of thinking, and the differences between the so-called basic and clinical sciences should diminish. At present, health professions students are interested in clinical courses and view the basic sciences as hurdles. If these sciences are to make their maximal contribution, they should be learned as they assist in the solution of clinical problems. If this approach to learning is used in teaching, there will be less reason for concern about the different cognitive backgrounds of students when they come to school.

5. New systems of ambulatory health care are not sufficient to improve quality of health services. They may improve access to the system but today, using any of the present organizational patterns, the outcome in terms of quality is determined more by the people involved and what happens at the point of contact than by the organization of the service. Any system can exclude persons, provide fewer than adequate resources, or extend those services. These factors affect quantity of service more than quality. Quality in health care, as in most other areas, rests primarily with the individuals involved.

6. The present system has in the past focused upon the central role of practitioners but is now moving in a direction of growing reliance on the system itself rather than on the individuals providing the services. This is a dangerous trend, for a system cannot guarantee quality if the individual service providers are not highly qualified. Quality care demands well-trained professionals, not poorly trained

auxiliaries. If we are to use physician assistants, for example, they must be good enough for the suburbs, not just for the ghettos.

7. In order to produce such providers, concentration on the fund of knowledge is not enough. In addition to knowledge, skills and emotional maturity are also necessary. It is required therefore that we make progress in the noncognitive areas. For a person to pass a conventional test and therefore acquire a license to practice in the health field does not assure quality. We need *qual*ifiers as well as *quan*tifiers as evaluative tools.

8. The popular notions about economics of health care erroneously attribute the rapid escalation in cost to single formulas like the number of hospital beds or the number of doctors per unit of population. In a period when there is rapid increase in the number of people being covered by medical insurance, it is at least misleading to lump all the payment in one figure and compare that amount with an earlier one. It is like discussing the cost of travel in terms of the number of airports. Instead, we should be discussing cost per unit of service delivered. In that case we would include not only the cost of caring for a patient with tuberculosis or manic depressive psychosis, but also the cost of a heart attack to the family of a patient who lives in a rural area, or the benefit to a ghetto community of having health services immediately available so that a day of work need not be lost each time medical care is required.

There is a cost of accessibility and a cost of quality. At some point decreased accessibility becomes a charge against quality. The notion of limiting the number of sophisticated facilities or of doctors may be logical if only the dollar cost is considered. This assumes that regulation and manipulation can be relied upon to assure quality care just as they can demonstrably prevent it. The present focus on reducing cost by limiting the availability of care is particularly unfair to consumers who have only recently been brought into the health care system. Economists and managers cannot reduce health care cost in a way which is fair and also preserves quality. The only reliable method of decreasing cost is to provide some incentive for moving provision of care to an earlier phase in the continuum, that is, from tertiary to secondary to primary to prevention.

Instead of reducing available services, economic forces must be used to push care in the cost effective direction, a striking contrast to the present system which makes tertiary care most profitable to providers. Such a change might be accomplished by providing chronic disease care in public hospitals and tertiary care on a cost reimbursable basis in the larger medical centers. At the least expensive end of the spectrum, preventive care and primary care would be supported on a fee-for-service basis providing enough profit to encourage providers to invest their major efforts in identifying and managing disease at this less expensive part of the spectrum. Disorders requiring secondary treatment (like appendectomies) would be placed in the fee-for-service or cost reimbursement category, depending on whether this or an earlier intervention represented the optimal management path. It is my belief that this approach is far more likely to reduce cost than merely withdrawing services or support from selected community areas or population groups.

9. Finally, caring is not assured by amount or type of payment; the amount or type of knowledge; the amount or type of facilities; or by regulations, laws, or the so-called system. And yet, for many people caring is the bottom line of health care. The most important factor in the development of the ability to care for others is the feeling that one has been cared for himself. Feelings of strong self-esteem, increased ability, or awareness of others' needs — while important ingredients — do not enable the individual to care to the same degree as a feeling that the caretaker himself was loved as a child and as an adult is respected, appreciated, and wanted in his present role. In other words, if you want health professionals really to care for others it is necessary to show that you care for them. We can't conduct polls which tell dentists we don't like them, and then expect those practitioners to have a caring attitude. You can't tell physicians that they are widely regarded as crooks, then expect them to devote themselves fully to caring for you. If you want people to care, you must insure that they feel cared for, that they feel respected and appreciated themselves. If society is not willing to pay this price to develop health providers who care, perhaps we should resort to the system used in some parts of Africa where health professionals provide the technical skill but the family provides most of the caring, whether a patient is inside or outside the hospital.

The danger that faces us is that we will choose between quality care for a few and mediocre care for all. This dilemma is unnecessary. The alternative is a multifaceted approach which chooses the most successful from the haves and the have-nots and judiciously combines government and free enterprise, knowledge and concern, standards and caring to provide the best for all. Racism, sexism, and poverty still remain the greatest enemies of quality *and* equality in health care and education. But as these enemies are overcome, it is incumbent upon the health professions educators to avoid creating new ones.

Comments, Questions, and Discussion

Following the address three University administrative officers were invited to comment. After a response from Dr. Elam more general discussion took place.

The invited discussants were John E. Corbally, president, University of Illinois; William J. Grove, vice-chancellor for academic affairs, University of Illinois at the Medical Center; and Helen K. Grace, dean of the College of Nursing, University of Illinois at the Medical Center. Alexander M. Schmidt, vice-chancellor for health services, University of Illinois at the Medical Center, served as moderator for the session.

President Corbally: First let me thank you, Dr. Elam, for a very stimulating presentation. We are all most grateful for what you have offered us.

In that presentation you noted that while we have reached a remarkably high level of achievement in the development of resources to deliver the best kind of health service it has been coupled with increasingly frequent expressions of disillusionment with the providers of those services. However, one might conclude that this mounting criticism merely reflects the importance of the health sciences and health professions and the fact that the expectations we have of them are very high. This may be an encouraging point of departure for further dialogue about the issues of improving both quality and equality in these fields.

You also spent some time in describing the different ways in which people think of equality: in terms of opportunity, access, numbers, and pay, among others. It seemed to me that you then went on to describe the five or six ways in which we might achieve quality. I have a feeling that we have as much trouble with different meanings of quality as we do with different meanings of equality. For example, when I go to see a physician I often feel better or worse after that visit, not so much in terms of what has been done for my physical health but in terms of how I have been treated — your caring comment. It may be that I could be fooled by a very bad physician who is a very fine human being and who kept making me feel good all the time, mentally, while I was slowly wasting away from some physical problem. So I might describe high quality in terms of the compassionate physician, whereas I am sure others might think in terms of skills in curing people. I would be interested in some comment on whether you feel there is as great a range of meanings in the area of quality as there is in the area of equality.

Vice-Chancellor Grove: It is difficult, after such a moving presentation, to bring oneself to break the spell. But I need to put before the group the record of the University of Illinois at the Medical Center with respect to minority representation. We have had a special program since 1969 to increase minority admissions, and the number of graduates as well. In 1970-71, 5.7 percent, or 153, members of the total student body were from minority groups. In 1978-79 that number had increased to 12.4 percent, or 550 students. Yet leaders of minority groups exhort us to do more — as we should.

Nonetheless, as I reflect upon thirty-nine years of experience on this campus, I note a great change in the race and sex of both student body and faculty. Thirty-nine years ago the rare minority student would probably have been classified, using the current terminology, as an Asian or Pacific Islander. There were essentially no black or Hispanic students and no faculty members from either group. Virtually all of the students and faculty were white and English was their native tongue. The few faculty members who spoke with a thick accent were generally refugees from Hitler's Germany. One of the things that continues to amaze me as I walk around the campus today is the contrast with 1940. Today we are of varied colors, have many native tongues, and represent both sexes.

This campus, particularly the College of Medicine, has had a long experience with mixed student cultures, even among the essentially all white male population of 1940. Then the contrasting backgrounds were those brought by students from downstate counties and from Cook County. The two populations were very different in their "level of success," to use your word. The policy of admitting students from Cook County and the remaining counties of the state in the same ratio as the population of Cook County to that of the other counties produced this contrast. Then, about 1950 the Illinois Agricultural Association and the Illinois State Medical Society initiated a recruitment program for individuals who would return to underserved areas to practice, and thus another set of backgrounds was introduced into the student population. In 1969 not only medicine but all of the colleges began to seek those from yet another group — minorities.

In spite of our careful selection of those best qualified within each of these groups, some of those selected are unable to meet established standards for graduation. And so faculty members in all of the colleges become discontented and say there must be a better way. In your paper, Dr. Elam, you suggested that perhaps we should change some of our modes of teaching; independent study and diversified tracks were two alternatives you proposed.

Because of the problems we are having in recruiting qualified students, and the external pressures to extend our commitment to minority groups, we have launched the Urban Health Program. One major thrust of that program is a long-term effort to improve the quality of applicants for admission to medical schools and colleges. To help us with that work we have recruited new staff members who are especially sensitive to these issues, and have invited community representatives to serve on citizen advisory groups. One of the problems which I perceive is that among those from the minority community, as well as among minority staff members, there seems to be disagreement about how best to approach the issues of quality and *in*equality. It seems to me that some reflect a segregationist view and others take an integrationist stand. I would like your reaction to whether I ought to dismiss that perception or whether it is real. If it is real, do you have any advice about how we should manage the differing views?

Dean Grace: Dr. Elam has clearly drawn the relationship between quality medical education, quality medical care, and issues of equality in both systems. He has noted, "It is only when we attempt a synthesis of the two that a solution of one side seems to confound the other." In reacting to this paper, I shall focus my remarks on a careful examination of these relationships. Additionally, I will attempt to place medical education and medical care within a broader framework.

First, it is important to consider the issues of quality in education. Dr. Elam has accurately noted that quality of educational programs is essentially assured by the selection of students most likely to be successful in memorizing and reiterating facts, and this achievement is indicated by test scores. Selection and performance criteria are unidimensional; those who perform best on preadmission examinations are the same students who do well on tests over the content areas of medical education. The faculty breathes a sigh of relief when students perform well, because it is then assumed that they will be "safe" practitioners. That students have not learned to relate with patients in a humanistic way or that their view of the world is circumscribed is not commonly deemed relevant or of great importance.

Turning to the medical care delivery system, Dr. Elam argues that quality is measured by externally imposed standards. Most frequently these standards are not based on outcomes of care but on certain fixed criteria, such as number of surgical cases of a particular type performed within a certain setting. The influence of the external reward system upon performance, the presence of an adequate number and variety of facilities and equipment, and the organization of the delivery system are identified by Dr. Elam as elements affecting the quality of care provided. Within this schema it is argued that the more highly sophisticated the system the better the care. Reiser, in tracing the development of technology in medical practice, notes, "Many modern physicians thus seem to order the value of medical evidence in a hierarchy: facts obtained through complex scientific procedures they regard as more accurate and germane to diagnosis than facts they detect through their own senses, which, in turn, they value more than facts disclosed by the patients' statements."[1] Specialization and the provision of care in the most technologically advanced setting, the hopsital, is valued as "best." The fit between the medical education system and what is defined as "quality" medical care is evident. Within this technological framework the medical system is judged to function satisfactorily. The more serious the illness of the patient, the better the medical care system functions; the more complex the technological aspects of care, the better. Conversely, the system functions at its worst in the area of health education, health maintenance, and illness detection. Linkage of patients into the health delivery network, continuity of care, development of care planning within a socioeconomic and cultural context are where the system works least well. But this system of medical education and medical care is embedded within the predominant American culture in which every problem has a specialist uniquely qualified to deal with it. Responsibility for management of problems is shifted from the individual, who sees himself as having no expertise, to the specialist, who is perceived to be all-knowing.

Dr. Elam argues that addressing issues of equality is the means of altering these qualitative orientations to medical education and medical care. The very same factors that have served as indicators of quality in medical education and medical care have resulted in large numbers of the population being considered as ineligible for access to medical education. Those who are judged least likely to succeed are those least oriented to test performance and rote memory, such as blacks, women, and non-English–speaking minorities. It is argued that inclusion of a broader range of students in medical education will aid in pursuing the issues of health service delivery to underserved communities and the aspects of health care not currently being addressed. With this as a focus, attention is placed upon identification of those

---

[1] Stanley Joel Reiser, *Medicine and the Reign of Technology,* Cambridge: Cambridge University Press, 1978, pg. 17.

most likely to be successful from a broader population base and modification of the curriculum to accommodate this diversified student group. It is argued that by providing a different context for the clinical practice component of the curriculum, this experience will carry over when the student enters the medical care delivery system as a practitioner. While this is certainly a valid argument, such a view begs many other confounding issues.

First, I must emphasize the importance of considering issues related to medical education in a broader context of health professions education. Currently, the burden for change in medical education and medical care is placed upon physicians alone, without realizing that solutions to the multifaceted and many-layered problems will require an array of health professionals working together to achieve some differing outcomes. Proposed solutions should be very carefully planned so that they do not inadvertently destroy some very real strengths in our current system. It is particularly important to assess the feasibility of change within the predominant societal framework. I firmly believe that there is a need for highly sophisticated medical specialists and a well-developed medical technology, and in altering the system I would hope that these qualitative aspects not be diminished. I firmly believe it is possible to alter the health delivery system to address issues of access, scope of care, and the promotion of health, while maintaining a highly sophisticated array of people and services for the acutely ill portion of the population. Both must be addressed without sacrificing one for the sake of the other.

But instead of placing the entire burden for change upon medical education and medical care, the whole array of health professionals and the contributions each can make to these goals need to be considered. I do not think the most valid use of highly prepared physicians is to be primary care providers in a variety of community settings and with a variety of patient populations. Dr. Elam has underscored the danger of an alternative that places ill-prepared individuals in those settings now underserved by professionals. But there is a middle position. Well-prepared nurse clinicians can provide superb services, in the community context, in the areas of health assessment, long-term care management, health education, and referral of patients into the medical care system. Nurses have the capabilities of addressing the issues of generalization and, linked appropriately into the network, can play a key role in the front lines of health care delivery. This does not diminish the physician's role, but instead complements his or her place in the total health care delivery system. Pharmacists and allied health professionals have their unique roles in a balanced system. Improvement of equality in health care can best be achieved if we address the issues collaboratively rather than unilaterally.

To achieve this it behooves us to find ways of addressing issues of equality both in education and in service delivery at the earliest stages of discussions. Too frequently each of us addresses the problems that we perceive unilaterally, without seeing how much easier the solutions might be if we respected the competence of each of the health professionals in the health delivery system and constructed our systems to utilize the multifaceted skills and talents of a variety of people. Instead, we make the assumption that one member of the team, the physician, is the only one with the responsibility or the capability of addressing the problems.

If this change in orientation to problem solving is a viable goal, it is important that it be built into the basic framework of health professions education. In the current education system, each member of the health professions disciplines is taught in a separate system. Nowhere in the educational process is there time (since we are so intent on seeing that students learn "facts") for students to learn to appreciate one another as bringing different areas of expertise and different orientations into the health care delivery arena. Role models of faculty in schools of medicine working with faculty in schools of nursing, for example, are extremely limited. The students pattern their behavior after that of teachers. Lacking such orientation as a basic component of their educational program, the graduates as they enter into practice have had no socialization into patterns of collaboration as the baseline of their work. As Dr. Elam has noted, development of ambulatory care as a basic component of the clinical practice experience is a key in developing this broader orientation to medical practice. I would argue that it is an appropriate beginning step. But I would also like to see settings in which nursing faculty, medical faculty, and faculty of other health disciplines collaborate in all aspects of health care delivery and thus establish the baseline of equality in both education and service delivery.

Dr. Elam: Thank you very much. I am flattered by your comments on my paper and pleased by the observations you have made. Let me begin my response, Dean Grace, by saying I absolutely agree with you that we can never solve the problem by approaching it from the point of view of one profession alone. My own program at Meharry is in fact one which trains nurse practitioners for the developing countries. We can't train their physicians on site and can only bring back a few to be trained here, so that limits us in terms of numbers, but I certainly agree with your view. However, there is a point of disagreement about how to educate health personnel to work together. I have tried several ways and have decided that if the goal is to assure interprofessional cooperation and understanding among nurses, physicians, psychologists, and social workers, for example, it is a mistake to start their training together. You must train each discipline independently long enough to develop an individual professional identity, then continue their training together. If they begin together, they never acquire quite enough of the necessary individual professional differences, and you create a situation in which a social worker, a nurse, and a psychiatrist are on the same team, but rather than being three different professions they seem like one, having failed to differentiate enough.

Dean Grace: I totally agree with you. That is why I stressed the importance of *faculty* working together.

Dr. Elam: Now let me turn to the question of whether the physician should do primary care. I think the most important sector of the whole health care system is disease prevention; a close second to that is primary care. When patients are very sick, they don't appreciate that fact. The person who has serious valvular heart disease wants a physician who can do something definitive about that defect. But how much more important it really is to have, for example, a program in the grade school that leads both children and parents to take the steps needed to prevent the valvulitis from developing. We all recognize that this is the principal point at which intervention should occur. For that reason I think it is very important to have people from all specialties involved in primary care: physicians, nurses, social workers, and psychologists should all play some part in that segment of the health care spectrum. I think it should also be the most profitable area, in monetary terms. Since we live in a society in which money is a motivating factor, primary care is where the payoff should be. Even better, put it in prevention. I haven't figured out how to do it, but that is really where the greatest profit should be earned. If it were, that is where practitioners would be. If we have nurses running primary care programs and no physicians involved, then primary care will somehow seem of only secondary importance, at least in the eyes of patients. I say this even though in Botswana that is exactly what we are doing: the nurses work in primary care, not the physicians. Nonetheless, even there the hospital has more prestige than primary care settings. I am convinced that both are needed.

Now let me turn to President Corbally's comment about the bad physician who makes you feel good. If a physician has neither good caring qualities nor good scientific qualities he is just incompetent and is not going to be around very long. If the practitioner taking care of you is a terrific human being but doesn't know anything, he really is a fraud, one who makes patients think he is doing something useful when he really isn't. The best example of that may be the chiropractor who often impresses patients through facade rather than substance. On the other hand, if the practitioner has a good scientific background but doesn't care for patients very well he is going to get sued. I think that in order to avoid being a fraud or getting sued you need to mix the caring and the scientific base. As a matter of fact Tinsley Harrison in *Your Future Health Care* attributes the improvement in medical education to two traditions: first, the development of medical schools in association with hospitals where teaching is centered around individual patients with spontaneous and formal training in small groups; second, the development of medical schools as integral parts of the University with an emphasis on medical science and research. These two traditions are usually identified by reference to William Osler and Abraham Flexner. Harrison says, "Because of the advances both in research and in education the quality of health care has risen sharply. This rise has occurred because of the application, both preventive and curative, of the new knowledge that first has to be acquired through research, and then disseminated through education. But this is not to say that either as regards service or education do we live in the best of all worlds."

My comment is intended to emphasize a belief that we must have in our educational programs both the scientific and the caring components. I am not certain that we are doing it very well, in part because we don't know very well how to facilitate the acquisition of caring but also because we offer the scientific part so early and base it on memory rather than on use of knowledge.

Dr. Grove asked whether it is true that there are people who see the approach to quality and equality in a segregationist mode and others who have an integrationist view. I believe that there are these two camps. Those who take the segregationist view are people who seek a political base. Individuals who take the integrationist approach have a different view of what is needed to effect change. If you look into the political world it is clear that for a minority person who wants to get elected rapidly the best place to live is in a minority community. However, a person who wants to get elected to represent a total population needs the support of all component groups, and living in a segregated community will not serve very well. The same thing is true in education. If you are trying to develop a system into which students can be admitted rapidly, a segregationist approach will be best. It was just such a system that was struck down by the Supreme Court — a system in which a certain number of places were reserved for minorities. But if you want a long-term solution to the problem this is not the way to go. Instead, it is necessary to find a way for everybody to compete, a way to choose individuals most likely to be successful in what needs to be done. That way is the most promising approach to both quality and equality. Personally I do not think that any school should follow the segregationist view, although I know that there are those who disagree with me. On the other hand, I do not think that any school can fairly develop a program in which only a small number of parameters are employed in the selection process, for that will inevitably produce an elite student body. That we must guard against.

President Corbally: Isn't the long-range solution one in which if there *is* one parameter, or two, or three, some limited number that does predict success as an "X" — physician, accountant, or whatever the profession for which students are being selected. Our homes, our families, our elementary schools, our secondary schools, and our society would develop in such a way that when students get to the point of selection, admission groups could use a small number of parameters, and could do so without being unfair to any individual because of the backgrounds they bring to the moment of selection.

Dr. Elam: I don't think that would be best *unless* we chose a parameter in keeping with what is needed at the end. For example, if you look at Medical College Admission Test scores and compare them with later achievement, those who have high scores do well in the first two years of medical school. On the other hand, if you look at admission interview assessments there is no correlation with how well they do the first two years. But if you compare these findings with how well individuals do in residency training, then you find that the ones who did the best on the interview perform best as residents. Which one, then, should we use, if we are to use only one: that which selects students who will do well in their first two years (who will surely pass the academic requirements but won't be good as physicians) or that which selects students who may have trouble in the first two years but if they make it through will be good doctors? In my opinion we should use both.

Vice-Chancellor Schmidt: Let me turn now to all of those who have been patiently listening to others' thoughts and questions. Please use this opportunity to talk with Dr. Elam.

Questioner: Dr. Elam, you said that the definition of quality is not critical but then went on to illustrate some of the elements that have been used in its identification, such as equal access and equal opportunity. All of these, however, can be used to weed out potential health providers along the way, and thus impede the achievement of equality as well as quality.

Dr. Elam: It is for just this reason that I think the health professions cannot afford to have a narrow view of equality. They must accept the fact that different groups of people will look at different aspects. As a matter of fact, there may be some people in this room who will never acknowledge that equality has been achieved until parity has been won: if the population has 10 percent of a particular group then 10 percent of the doctors must come from that group. It will surely be a long time before such a goal is reached, but the health professions must accept the fact that this is one of the definitions of equality by which they will be measured. My comment was intended to emphasize the importance of recognizing all these definitions of equality so that in all programs they will be considered.

Questioner: What is being done in the admissions process to identify in applicants the personal characteristics you have emphasized, things that go beyond mere scholastic achievement?

Dr. Elam: Research indicates that there is a correlation between how well people do as doctors, as reported by their residency supervisors, and how well they did on the admissions interview. This research has been repeatedly confirmed, and I think most schools now require an interview as part of the selection process. As more and more schools take seriously the findings from this procedure I think we will more and more take into account these noncognitive factors.

However, it is equally important for schools to *care for* the students they admit. If the way students were treated some years ago is compared to the way they are treated in medical school now, I tell you that there is a difference, manifested by far greater efforts to treat students as responsible adults who need caring as well as facts. If we do not behave this way then we are unlikely to develop doctors who are going to care for patients. The major problem that I see in this area has to do with the institutional reward system. Faculty members are not often rewarded for caring for students but for doing research, writing papers, even serving on committees, a variety of things which do not reinforce a faculty commitment to this caring value and practice. Students have discovered this and try to remedy the institutional failure by giving various prizes to faculty who do care.

Those are two ways in which I think we can try to encourage caring. You can't teach students to empathize; you can't simply lecture about how to empathize; you must provide an atmosphere that makes students want to empathize.

Questioner: Do the various schools and colleges on this campus use the interview as part of the admissions process?

Vice-Chancellor Grove: I can only speak with any degree of authority about the College of Medicine. A number of years ago the interview system was discontinued because it was kind of a travesty on the selection process, since those who interviewed did not know whether they were screening or recruiting. It tended to be a situation in which the interviewer concluded that those who most resembled his own personality must be good candidates. About three years ago the admissions committee began an intensive study of the interview process, to determine how an interview system might be set up which would approach objectivity and what such a system would cost. A year and a half ago steps toward implementation of such a system were taken. It is my understanding that it will be in place for students who will be selected for the entering class in 1980. The other colleges do interview some students.

President Corbally: I can add what I think is a sad commentary on some of these efforts. It reflects the effect of our current tendency to sue on almost every issue. As surprising as it may seem to many people, the greatest pressure the University of Illinois receives for admission is to the College of Veterinary Medicine at Urbana. It is the only such college in the state, and there are only about twenty veterinary colleges in the whole country. If you don't have one in your state or if you are not in a state which has a contract with a college of veterinary medicine in another state it is virtually impossible to get in. Obviously the alternatives are very limited. Only recently has it been possible to go to Guadalajara.

Therefore applicants feel very intensely about these limited opportunities, and we began to have a growing number of lawsuits about admission decisions, particularly those related to subjective judgments. Thus, we have been pushed more and more into making admissions decisions on the basis of quantitative data that can be defended as being objective, even though we all know that numbers can be equally unreliable. This has led admissions committees in veterinary medicine to decrease the weight given to the interview as a part of the admissions process because the interview was most vulnerable to the charge that it led to discriminatory decisions. For example, it is charged that interviews discriminate against the person from a big city who did not have opportunity to become as familiar with animals as the person from the rural area, and therefore was at a disadvantage in the interview. The same problem is appearing elsewhere. Law schools increasingly take grade-point-hour ratio and the LSAT, add them together, rank candidates, and draw a line.

That is a countereffect to some of the efforts to broaden admissions criteria. But I think there is need for a great deal of effort to restudy how we can better make these decisions, knowing that, while they are all subjective, they have to be made as carefully, as honestly, and as closely related to the purpose as possible. It is surely useful to seek ways to get back to interviews and to other kinds of measures which are not easily quantifiable.

Vice-Chancellor Schmidt: It is also important to recall that Dr. Elam mentioned that our academic system seems not to be rewarding faculty who care about students. Neither has it been rewarding the role model of the great physician. As I read medical history, about the Soma

Weisses and the others who were so inspirational in the way they treated patients and how they cared for people, it seems our modern technological society has gone a little away from providing that kind of role model.

Questioner: In the course of your lecture you noted the importance of dealing both with the unknown frontiers and with providing a caring environment for students as well as patients. Perhaps this suggests that we need two types of health professionals. On the one hand we need some who will be professionally discontented, always trying to prove something, who have perhaps had unfortunate childhoods or frustrating school years but who will become the individuals who devote themselves to exploring those frontiers. At the same time there is surely no question that we need the other, with the background of nurture, who will be caring and sympathetic practitioners.

Dr. Elam: I certainly agree that we need to stimulate and develop great researchers, although I don't know how to do it. I am pleased to know you recognize that, at the Freudian level, the reason people are involved in research may be that they are trying to discover something about themselves. Freud had some words about what part their sexual curiosity played in arousing their interest in research. I don't know exactly how you do this, but however we do it I think we should. We must take into account, though, that of the great discoveries in medicine many have occurred because faculty/teachers/researchers were concerned with people. Some discoveries have surely been made by people who spent their whole lives working with mice, and we should not discount the fact some faculty members don't like to work with people. But if you look at the recent big discoveries, they were made by those who were concerned with people. I think we need to find better ways to get the two together. However, developing researchers is a very important activity. I say that we don't know how to do it because I see so many researchers who are simply compulsive types. Maybe that is the way it should be, but we also need some researchers who are concerned, who are innovative, who come up with new ideas, not just the compulsive ones who keep working until they get to be full professors.

James G. March has devoted his career to the study of administration and leadership in society. He is professor of sociology and political science and Fred H. Merrill Professor of Management at Stanford University. Although Dr. March deals with administrative theory, he is not without administrative practice. He was the founding dean of the School of Social Sciences of the University of California at Irvine.

Dr. March received his bachelor of arts degree in political science in 1949 from the University of Wisconsin, and his master's degree and doctorate in political science from Yale University. He's had fellowships from the Social Science Research Council and the Center for Advanced Study in the Behavioral Sciences. He has served his discipline well and widely as editor, board member, officer and consultant to business, government, universities, non-profit corporations, military organizations and professional associations.

The seventh Henry Lecture was presented September 25, 1980, at the University of Illinois at Urbana-Champaign.

How We Talk and How We Act:
Administrative Theory and Administrative Life[*]

By James G. March
Merrill Professor of Management
Stanford University

It is a special pleasure for me to be here today. Although I have lived longer in California than anywhere else, and California life unquestionably agrees with me, I am by birth, rearing, and instincts a midwesterner with the usual midwestern prejudices. So I am glad to be back. It is particularly a pleasure to be asked to give the David D. Henry Lecture.

As a faculty member, I know how dangerous it is to praise administrators in their own organizations. Administration is the art of disappointing people, and those who have been disappointed do not always see administrative beauty in their tormentors; but it seems to me that the University of Illinois has been fortunate in having several senior administrators in recent years who have combined administrative skill with academic values and a commitment to scholarship. The combination has allowed them both to be administrators and to write about administration with grace and distinction. I think particularly of David Henry, Jack Peltason, and Jack Corbally. To talk about the relation between administrative leadership and administrative thought in an institution with such a distinguished history of both is an honor for me.

---

[*] This paper was given as the David D. Henry Lecture on Administration at the University of Illinois at Urbana-Champaign, September 25, 1980. It is based, in part, on work done jointly with Michael Cohen, Martha Feldman, Daniel Levinthal, James C. March, and Johan P. Olsen, and supported by grants from the Spencer Foundation, the National Institute of Education, and the Hoover Institution.

I am not an administrator. I believe I am only the second person without experience as a college president to be invited to deliver the David D. Henry Lecture. I am a student of organizations and administration, and it is from that point of view that I talk. Nevertheless, I hope that some comments from the ivory tower may be marginally useful to the real world of administration. Students of organizations are secretaries to people who live in organizations. Much of our time is spent talking to people in administrative roles, recording their behavior, and trying to develop descriptions of organizational life that fit common administrative experiences into a larger metaphor of organizational theory. As best we can, we try to make sense of what we see.

Making sense of organizational life is complicated by the fact that organizations exist on two levels. The first is the level of action where we cope with the environment we face; the second is the level of interpretation where we fit our history into an understanding of life. The level of action is dominated by experience and learned routines; the level of interpretation is dominated by intellect and the metaphors of theory. Ordinary administrative life is a delicate combination of the two levels. Managers act. They make decisions, establish rules, issue directives. At the same time, they interpret the events they see. They try to understand their own behavior, as well as that of others, in terms of theories that they (and others) accept. They try to present themselves in understandable, even favorable, terms. They try to improve the way they act by contemplating its relation to the way they talk, and they try to modify their talk by considering how they act.

The process has elegance, but it also has traps. The interweaving of experience and theory often makes it difficult for the student of administration to disentangle the events of organizational life from the theories about those events which participants have. The same interweaving complicates the ways in which administrators learn from their experience to improve their organizations. I want to explore some aspects of those complications today. My intentions are not grand. I want to talk about some parts of administrative theory and administrative life, about the implications of recent thinking on organizations, and particularly about the possibility that some of our administrative precepts — the way we talk — may sometimes be less sensible than our administrative behavior — the way we act.

Classical perspectives on administrative leadership are rich enough and varied enough to make any effort to describe them in broad terms ill-informed. Nevertheless, there is a relatively standard portrayal of organizations and their leaders that is easily recognized and is implicit in most of our administrative theories. Without attempting to represent those theories in a comprehensive way, I want to focus on four assumptions of administrative thought that are important both to contemporary administrative action and to recent research on administrative life:

Assumption 1: The rigidity of organizations. In the absence of decisive and imaginative action by administrative leaders, organizations resist change.

Assumption 2: The heterogeneity of managers. Top managers vary substantially in their capabilities, and organizations that identify and reward distinctively able administrative leaders prosper.

Assumption 3: The clarity of objectives. Intelligent administrative action presupposes clear goals, precise plans, and unambiguous criteria for evaluation.

Assumption 4: The instrumentality of action. The justification for administrative action lies in the substantive outcomes it produces.

These assumptions permeate both our writings and our talk about organizations and administration. Although it is certainly possible to find counterexamples in the literature, they are part of generally received administrative doctrine. Moreover, they are not foolish. They reflect considerable good sense. One difficulty with them, however, is that they appear to capture only part of our experience. Most studies of administrative life present a somewhat different vision of administrative roles. Although there is a tendency for some biographers of particular leaders to surround administrative life with grandeur, most studies and most reports from administrators present a different picture of what administrators do. Administrative life seems to be filled with minor things, short-time horizons, and seemingly pointless (and endless) commitments. The goals of an organization seem to be unclear and changing. Experience seems to be obscure. Life is filled with events of little apparent instrumental consequence. The ways in which administrative theory leads us to talk about administrative life seem to be partially inconsistent with the ways in which we have experienced and observed it.

Such an inconsistency is neither surprising nor, by itself, disturbing. Tensions between theory and experience are important sources of development for both. But in this case, I think our theories lead us astray in some important ways. In order to examine that thought, I want to note some observations about organizational life drawn from recent research. First, some observations about change; second, some observations about clarity; third, some observations about managers and managerial incentives; and fourth, some observations about instrumentality in administrative life. Taken together, these observations suggest some modest modifications in our assumptions of management.

Organizations and change

Recent literature on organizations often details the ways that hopes for change are frustrated by organizational behavior. The contrariness of organizations in confronting sensible efforts to change them fills our stories and our research. What most of those experiences tell us, however, is not that organizations are rigid and inflexible. Rather, they picture organizations as impressively imaginative. Organizations change in response to their environments, including their managements; but they rarely change in a way that fulfills the intentional plan of a single group of actors. Sometimes organizations ignore clear policies; sometimes they pursue them more forcefully than was intended. Sometimes they protect policymakers from the follies of foolish policies; sometimes they do not. Sometimes they stand still when we want them to move. Sometimes they move when we want them to stand still.

Organizational tendencies to frustrate arbitrary administrative intention, however, should not be confused with rigidity. Organizations change frequently. They adopt new products, new procedures, new objectives, new postures, new styles, new personnel, new beliefs. Even in a short perspective, the changes are often large. Some of them are sensible; some are not. Bureaucratic organizations are not always efficient. They can be exceptionally obtuse. Change is ubiquitous in organizations; and most change is the result neither of extraordinary organizational processes or forces, nor of uncommon imagination, persistence, or skill. It is a result of relatively stable processes that relate organizations to their environments. Organizational histories are written in dramatic form, and the drama reflects something important about the orchestration and mythology of organizational life; but substantial change results easily from the fact that many of the actions by an organization follow standard rules that are conditional on the environment. If economic, political, or social contexts change rapidly, organizations will change rapidly and routinely.

In such a spirit, recent efforts to understand organizations as routine adaptive systems emphasize six basic perspectives for interpreting organizational action:

1. Action can be seen as the application of standard operating procedures or other rules to appropriate situations. The terms of reference are duties, obligations, and roles. The model is a model of evolutionary selection.

2. Action can be seen as problem solving. The terms of reference are alternatives, consequences, and preferences. The model is one of intended rational choice.

3. Action can be seen as stemming from past learning. The terms

of reference are actions and experiences. The model is one of trial and error learning.

4. Action can be seen as resulting from conflict among individuals or groups. The terms of reference are interests, activation, and resources. The model is one of politics — bargaining and power.

5. Action can be seen as spreading from one organization to another. The terms of reference are exposure and susceptibility. The model is one of diffusion.

6. Action can be seen as stemming from the mix of intentions and competencies found in organizational actors. The terms of reference are attitudes, abilities, and turnover. The model is one of regeneration.

These standard processes of organizational action are understandable and mostly reliable. Much of the time they are adaptive. They facilitate organizational survival. Sometimes organizations decline, and sometimes they die. Sometimes the changes that are produced seem little connected either to the intentions of organizational actors or to the manifest problems facing an organization. A propensity to change does not assure survival, and the processes of change are complicated by a variety of confusions and surprises. Solutions sometimes discover problems rather than the other way around. Organizations imitate each other, but innovations and organizations change in the process. Environments are responded to, but they are also affected. The efforts of organizations to adapt are entangled with the simultaneous efforts of individuals and larger systems of organizations. In these ways, the same processes that sustain the dull day-to-day activities of an organization produce unusual events.

These six perspectives portray an organization as coping with the environment routinely, actively adapting to it, avoiding it, seeking to change it, comprehend it, and contain it. An organization is neither unconditionally rigid nor unconditionally malleable; it is a relatively complicated collection of interests and beliefs acting in response to conflicting and ambiguous signals received from the environment and from the organization, acting in a manner that often makes sense and usually is intelligent. Organizations evolve, solve problems, learn, bargain, imitate, and regenerate. Under a variety of circumstances, the processes are conservative. That is, they tend to maintain stable relations, sustain existing rules, and reduce differences among similar organizations. But the fundamental logic is not one of stability in behavior; it is one of adaptation. The processes are stable; the resulting actions are not.

Organizations change routinely and continually; and the effectiveness of an organization in responding to its environment, as well as much of the effectiveness of management, is linked to the effectiveness of routine processes. As a result, much of the job of an administrator involves the mundane work of making a bureaucracy work. It is filled with activities quite distant from those implied in a conception of administration as heroic leadership. It profits from ordinary competence and a recognition of the ways in which organizations change by modest modifications of routines rather than by massive mucking around. Studies of managerial time and behavior consistently show an implicit managerial recognition of the importance of these activities. The daily activities of a manager are rather distant from grand conceptions of organizational leadership. Administrators spend time talking to people about minor things, making trivial decisions, holding meetings with unimportant agendas, and responding to the little irritants of organizational life. Memoirs of administrators confirm the picture of a rewarding life made busy by large numbers of inconsequential things.

These observations describe administrative life as uncomfortably distant from the precepts of administrative theory and from hopes for personal significance. They have led to efforts to change the ways managers behave. Numerous training programs attempt to teach managers to bring their personal time allocation closer to the ideal. They provide procedures designed to increase the time for decision making, planning, thinking, and the other things that appear more characteristic of theories of administration than of administrative jobs. These efforts may be mistakes. Making bureaucracy work involves effectiveness in executing a large number of little things. Making bureaucracies change involves attention to the minor routines by which things happen. Rules need to be understood in order to be interpreted or broken; simple breakdowns in the flow of supplies need to be minimized; telephones and letters need to be answered; accounts and records need to be maintained.

The importance of simple competence in the routines of organizational life is often overlooked when we sing the grand arias of management, but effective bureaucracies are rarely dramatic. They are administrative organizations that require elementary efficiency as a necessary condition for quality. Efficiency as a concept has been subject to considerable sensible criticism on the grounds that it is either meaningless or misleading if we treat it independently of the objectives being pursued. The point is well taken as a critique of the "cult of efficiency," but it is much too simple if we take it as an assertion that all, or even most, efforts in an administrative organization need a clear specification of global goals to be done well. An administrative organization combines large numbers of tasks into some kinds of meaningful combinations, but much of the effectiveness of the combination depends on the relatively automatic, local correction of local inefficiencies without continuous attention to the "big picture."

Much of what distinguishes a good bureaucracy from a bad one is how well it accomplishes the trivia of day-to-day relations with clients and day-to-day problems in maintaining and operating its technology. Accomplishing these trivia may involve considerable planning, complex coordination, and central direction, but it is more commonly linked to the effectivenes of large numbers of people doing minor things competently. As a result, it is probably true that the conspicuous differences around the world in the quality of bureaucratic performance are due primarily to variance in the competence of the ordinary clerk, bureaucrat, and lower manager, and to the effectiveness of routine procedures for dealing with problems at a local level. This appears to be true of armies, factories, postal services, hotels, and universities.

Organizations and ambiguous preferences

The classical administrator acts on the basis of knowledge about objectives. Goals are presumed to be clear — or it is presumed to be a responsibility of administration to make them clear. Administrative life often seems to be filled with ambiguous preferences and goals, and this becomes particularly conspicuous as one nears the top of an organization. Objectives are hard to specify in a way that provides precise guidance. That is not to say that they are completely unknown or that all parts are equally obscure. Administrative goals are often unclear; when we try to make them clear, they often seem unacceptable.

Goal ambiguity is particularly troubling to a conception of rational administrative action. As we normally conceive it, rational action involves two kinds of guesses: guesses about future consequences and guesses about future preferences for those consequences. We try to imagine the future outcomes that will result from our present actions, and we try to imagine how we will evaluate those outcomes when they occur. Neither guess is necessarily easy. Anticipating future consequences of present decisions is often subject to substantial error. Anticipating future preferences is often confusing. Theories of rational choice are primarily theories of these two guesses and how we deal with their complications. Theories of choice under uncertainty emphasize the complications of guessing future consequences. Theories of choice under ambiguity emphasize the complications of guessing future preferences.

In standard prescriptive theories of choice:

Preferences are relevant. Prescriptive theories of choice require that action be taken in terms of preferences, that decisions be consistent with objectives in the light of information about the probable consequences of alternatives for valued outcomes.

Preferences are stable. With few exceptions, prescriptive theories of choice require that tastes be stable. Current action is taken in terms of current preferences. The implicit assumption is that preferences will be unchanged when the outcomes of current actions are realized.

Preferences are consistent. Prescriptive theories of choice allow mutually inconsistent preferences only insofar as they can be made irrelevant by the absence of scarcity or by the specification of tradeoffs.

Preferences are precise. Prescriptive theories of choice eliminate ambiguity about the extent to which a particular outcome will satisfy preferences, at least insofar as possible resolutions of ambiguity might affect the choice.

Preferences are exogenous. Prescriptive theories of choice presume that preferences, by whatever process they may be created, are not themselves affected by the choices they control.

Each of these theoretical features of proper preferences seems inconsistent with some observations of administrative behavior. Administrators often ignore their own, fully conscious preferences in making decisions. They follow rules, traditions, hunches, and the advice and actions of others. Preferences often change over time in such a way that predicting future preferences is often difficult. Preferences are often inconsistent. Managers and others in organizations are often aware of the extent to which some of their preferences conflict with others of their preferences, yet they do nothing to resolve the conflict. Many preferences are stated in forms that lack precision. It is difficult to make them reliably operational in evaluating possible outcomes. While preferences are used to choose among actions, it is often also true that actions and experiences with their consequences affect preferences. Preferences are determined partly endogenously.

It is possible, of course, that such portrayals of administrative behavior are perverse. They may be perverse because they systematically misrepresent the actual behavior of administrators, or they may be perverse because the administrators they describe are, insofar as the description applies, stupid. It is also possible that the description is accurate and the behavior is intelligent, that the ambiguous way administrators sometimes deal with preferences is, in fact, sensible. If such a thing can be imagined, then perhaps we treat preferences inadequately in administrative theory.

The disparity between administrative objectives, as they appear in administrative theory, and administrative objectives, as we observe them in organizational life, has led to efforts to "improve" the way administrators act. These characteristically emphasize the importance of goal clarity and of tying actions clearly to prior objectives. Deviations from the goal precision anticipated by decision theory have been treated as errors to be corrected. The strategy has led to important advances in management, and it has had its successes. But it also has had failures. Stories of disasters attributable to the introduction of decision technology are clichés of recent administrative experience.

As a result, students of administrative theory have been led to ask whether it is possible that goal ambiguity is not always a defect to be eliminated from administration, whether perhaps it may sometimes reflect a form of intelligence that is obscured by our models of rationality. For example, there are good reasons for moderating an enthusiasm for precise performance measures in organizations. The introduction of precision into the evaluation of performance involves a trade-off between the gains in outcomes attributable to closer articulation between action and measured objectives and the losses attributable to misrepresentation of goals, reduced motivation for development of goals, and concentration of effort on irrelevant ways of beating the index. Whether we are considering a performance evaluation scheme for managers or a testing procedure for students, there is likely to be a difference between the *maximum* clarity of goals and the *optimum* clarity.

The complications of performance measures, are, however, only an illustration of the general issue of goal ambiguity in administrative action. In order to examine the more general issue, we probably need to ask why an intelligent administrator might deliberately choose (or sensibly learn) to have ambiguous goals. In fact, rationalizing ambiguity is neither difficult nor novel, but it depends on perspectives somewhat more familiar to human understanding as it is found in literature, philosophy, and ordinary experience than as we see it in our theories of administration and choice. For example:

> Many administrators engage in activities designed to manage their own preferences. These activities make little sense from the point of view of a conception of action that assumes administrators know what they want and will want, or a conception that assumes wants are morally equivalent. But ordinary human actors sense that they might come to want something they should not, or that they might make unwise or inappropriate choices under the influence of fleeting, but powerful, desires if they do not control the development of preferences or buffer action from preferences.

Many administrators are both proponents for preferences and observers of the process by which preferences are developed and acted upon. As observers of the process by which their beliefs have been formed and evoked, they recognize the good sense in perceptual and moral modesty.

Many administrators maintain a lack of coherence both within and among personal desires, social demands, and moral codes. Though they seek some consistency, they appear to see inconsistency as a normal, and necessary, aspect of the development and clarification of values.

Many administrators are conscious of the importance of preferences as beliefs independent of their immediate action consequences. They accept a degree of personal and social wisdom in ordinary hypocrisy.

Many administrators recognize the political nature of rational argument more clearly than the theory of choice does. They are unwilling to gamble that God made clever people uniquely virtuous. They protect themselves from cleverness by obscuring the nature of their preferences; they exploit cleverness by asking others to construct reasons for actions they wish to take.

If these characteristics of ambiguous preferences processing by administrators make sense under rather general circumstances, our administrative theories based on ideas of clarity in objectives do not make as much sense as we sometimes attribute to them. Not only are they descriptively inadequate, they lead to attempts to clarify things that serve us better unclarified. Some of our standard dicta that managers should define and pursue clear objectives need to be qualified by a recognition that clarity is sometimes a mistake.

Organizations, managerial ambitions, and managerial incentives

In most conceptions of administration, administrators are assumed to be ambitious for promotion, position, and success. Managerial incentive schemes are efforts to link such personal ambitions of managers with the goals of the organization so that the behavior of self-interested managers contributes to achieving organizational objectives. As you move toward the top of an organization, however, some things happen that confuse ambition. Promotions are filters through which successful managers pass. Assuming that all promotions are based on similar attributes, each successive filter further refines the pool, reducing variation among managers. On attributes the organization considers important, vice-presidents are likely to be significantly more homogeneous than first-level managers. In addition, as we move up the organization, objectives usually become more conflicting and more ambiguous. Exactly what is expected of a manager sometimes seem obscure and changing, and it becomes harder to attribute specific outcomes to specific managerial actions.

Thus, as we move up the organization, evaluation procedures become less and less reliable, and the population of managers becomes more and more homogeneous. The joint result is that the noise level in evaluation approaches the variance in the pool of managers. At the limit, one vice-president cannot be reliably distinguished from another; and quality distinctions among top executives, however consistent with their records, are less likely to be justified than distinctions made at a lower level. Toward the top of an organization, it is difficult to know unambiguously that a particular manager makes a difference. Notice that this is not the same as suggesting that management is unimportant. Management may be extremely important even though managers are indistinguishable. It is hard to tell the difference between two different light bulbs also; but if you take all light bulbs away, it is difficult to read in the dark. What is hard to demonstrate is the extent to which high-performing managers (or light bulbs that endure for an exceptionally long time) are something more than one extreme end of a probability distribution of results generated by essentially equivalent individuals.

Because it has such properties, a mobility system in an organization is a hierarchy of partial lotteries in which the expected values of the lotteries increase as we move up the organization, but control over their outcomes declines. Of course, if the objective is to recruit ambitious and talented people into management, it may not matter whether potential managers are able to control outcomes precisely, as long as the expected values of the games are higher than other opportunities. Ambitious people will seek such careers even if they believe — which they may not — that the outcomes are chance. What is less clear is exactly what kind of managerial behavior will be stimulated by management lotteries.

At the heart of a managerial promotion and reward scheme is normally some measure of managerial performance. Managers are seen as improving organizational outcomes by trying to improve their own measured performance, but every index of performance is an invitation to cleverness. Long before reaching the top, an intelligent manager learns that some of the more effective ways of improving measured performance have little to do with improving product, service, or technology. A system of rewards linked to precise measures is not an incentive to perform well; it is an incentive to obtain a good score. At the same time, since managers are engaged in a lottery in which it is difficult to associate specific outcomes with specific managerial behavior, it becomes important to be able to say "I did the things a good manager should do." We develop a language for describing good managers and bad ones, and individual managers are able to learn social norms of management. Not all managers behave in exactly the same way, but they all learn the language, expectations, and styles. They are socialized into managerial roles.

These analyses of the consequences of managerial incentives at the top seem inconsistent with the way we talk about leadership in organizations. In effect, we now have two contending theories of how things happen in organizations. The first is considerably influenced by stories of great figures — Catherine the Great, Bismarck, Alfred Sloan — and elaborated by the drama of success and failure of individuals in bureaucratic settings. It portrays administration in relatively heroic ways. Such portrayals lead us to attribute a large share of the variance in organizational outcomes to special properties of specific individual managers. They are comfortably reassuring in the major role they assign to administrative leadership, but they seem to describe a world rather far from administrative experience or research.

The second theory (filled with metaphors of loose coupling, organized anarchy, and garbage can decision processes) seems to describe administrative reality better, but it appears uncomfortably pessimistic about the significance of administrators. Indeed, it seems potentially pernicious even if correct. Consider two general types of errors a manager might make in assessing the importance of intentional actions in controlling organizational outcomes. A manager might come to believe in considerable personal control over outcomes when, in fact, that control does not exist. A "false positive" error. Such a belief would lead to (futile) attempts to control events, but it would not otherwise affect results. Alternatively, a manager might come to believe that significant personal control is not possible when, in fact, it is. A "false negative" error. Such a belief would lead to self-confirming withdrawal from efforts to be effective. Either type of error is possible; but the social costs of the first seem small, relative to the second. Given a choice, we would generally prefer to err on the side of making false positive errors in assessing human significance, rather than false negative errors.

Perhaps fortunately, organizational life assures a managerial bias toward belief in managerial importance. Top managers are not random managers; they are successful managers. They rise to the top on the basis of a series of successful experiences. We know that individuals often find it easy to believe that successes in their lives are attributable to their talents and choices, while failures are more due to bad luck or malevolence. Promotion to the top on the basis of successes at lower levels results in top level executives believing in the possibility of substantial intentional control over organizational events. Even though their experiences might have led managers to such beliefs erroneously, managerial experience is likely to be subjectively very persuasive. In effect, the system of managerial mobility is designed to make managers much more resistant to false beliefs in impotence than to false beliefs in control. Administrative experience, as well as managerial self-esteem, will usually give managers a greater sense of personal importance and uniqueness than the second theory suggests.

In fact, there is a third theory; and it is probably closer to the truth than either of the others. In this third view, managers *do* affect the ways in which organizations function. But as a result of the process by which managers are selected, motivated, and trained, variations in managers do not reliably produce variations in organizational outcomes. In such a conception, administrators are vital as a class but not as individuals. Administration *is* important, and the many things that administrators do are essential to keeping the organization functioning; but if those vital things are only done when there is an unusually gifted individual at the top, the organization will not thrive. What makes an organization function well is the density of administrative competence, the kind of selection procedures that make all vice-presidents look alike from the point of view of their probable success, and the motivation that leads managers to push themselves to the limit.

Earlier, I used the analogy of a light bulb. I think it is a good analogy. If the manufacture of light bulbs is so unreliable that only a few actually work, you will not be able to do much reading. On the other hand, if light bulbs are reliable, you can read whenever you want to, but you won't much care which light bulb you use. One problem with some conventional administrative thought is that it encourages us to glorify an organization that finds the unique working light bulb in a large shipment of defective bulbs, rather than an organization that persistently produces a supply of nearly indistinguishable good bulbs. It is the latter organization that functions better.

Organizations, rituals, and symbols

Administrators and administrative decisions allocate scarce resources and are thereby of considerable social and individual importance, but decisions in organizations and the administration of them are important beyond their outcomes. They are also arenas for exercising social values, for displaying authority and position, and for exhibiting proper behavior and attitudes with respect to a central ideological construct of modern Western civilization — the concept of intelligent choice. Bureaucratic organizations are built on ideas of rationality, and rationality is built on ideas about the way decisions should be made. Indeed, it would be hard to find any institution in modern society more prototypically committed to systematic, rational action than a formal organization.

Thus, administrative action in an organization is a performance in which administrators try to behave in a normatively praiseworthy way. Making intelligent decisions is important, but the verification of intelligence in decision making is often difficult. As a result, it often becomes heavily procedural. For example, in the usual scenario for administrative performance, the gathering of information is not simply a basis for action; it is a representation of competence and a reaffirmation of personal virtue. Command of information and information sources enhances perceived competence and inspires confidence. The belief that more information characterizes better decisions and defensible decision processes engenders a conspicuous consumption of information. Information is flaunted but not used, collected but not considered.

Ideas about proper administrative behavior diffuse through a population of organizations and change over time. What makes a particular procedure appropriate for one manager is that it is being used in other successful organizations by other successful managers. What makes an administrative innovation new and promising is that it has been adopted by other organizations that are viewed as being intelligently innovative. Managerial procedures spread from successful organizations to unsuccessful ones, as the latter try to present themselves as equivalent to the former; and the signal a particular procedure provides is gradually degraded by its adoption by organizations that are not "well-managed" or "progressive," thus stimulating the invention of new procedures.

This competition among managers and organizations for legitimacy and standing is endless. As managers attempt to establish and maintain reputations through the symbols of good management, social values are sustained and elaborated. For symbols of administrative competence are, of course, symbols simultaneously of social efficacy. Belief in the appropriateness of administrative actions, the process by which they are taken, and the roles played by the various actors involved is a key part of a social structure. It is not only important to decision makers that they be viewed as legitimate; it is also useful to society that leaders be imagined to control organizational outcomes and to act in a way that can be reconciled with a sense of human control over human destiny.

Ritual acknowledgement of managerial importance and appropriateness is part of a social ceremony by which social life is made meaningful and acceptable under conditions that would otherwise be problematic. For example, managerial capabilities for controlling events are likely to be more immediately obvious to managers than to others in the organization. Since most of the managers with whom managers must deal are themselves successful managers, the problem is somewhat concealed from daily managerial experience. Many of the people whom we see in administration, particularly in a growing organization, are people who see themselves as successful; but there are others, less conspicuous, who do not derive the same prejudices from their own experience. So, we construct various myths of management. The same mobility process that encourages top managers in a belief in their own control over events tends to teach some others that managerial successes and the events associated with them are more due to luck or corruption.

The stories, myths, and rituals of management are not merely a way some people fool other people or a waste of time. They are fundamental to our lives. We embrace the mythologies and symbols of life and could not otherwise easily endure. Executive behavior and management procedures contribute to myths about management that become the reality of managerial life and reinforce a belief in a human destiny subject to intentional human control. They may not be essential to such a belief — it is reinforced in many subtle ways throughout society — but executive rituals and executive life are parts of that large mosaic of mutually supporting myths by which an instrumental society brings hope and frustration to individual lives. Since managerial rituals are important to our faith, and our faith is important to the functioning of organizations as well as the broader social and political order, these symbolic activities of administration are central to its success.

Most administrators seem ambivalent about symbol management. On the one hand, they recognize that they spend considerable time trying to sustain beliefs in the intelligence, coherence, importance, and uniqueness of their organizations (and themselves). At the same time, however, they seem to view the activity as either somewhat illegitimate or as an imposition on more important things — such as decision making, directing, or coordinating. They treat the rituals of administration as necessary, but they talk about them as a waste of time.

Partly, of course, the ambivalence is itself socially dictated. In a society that emphasizes instrumentality as much as Western society does, leaders would be less acceptable if they were to acknowledge the ritual activities of their jobs as central. One of their key symbolic responsibilities is to maintain an ideology that denies the legitimacy of symbol maintenance. Thus, they tend to do it but to deny they do it, or to bemoan the fact that they must do it. It is a careful dance along a narrow beam, and there is the possibility of much grace in it. But the elegance of the dance probably depends on a fine modulation between talk and action, as well as some administrative consciousness of the meaning of the dance. In order to achieve that consciousness, we probably need to recognize the ambivalence and to encourage administrators to see how the activities in which they participate are an essential part of a larger social ritual by which they, as well as others in society, reaffirm purpose and order in a potentially disorderly world.

Many managers, of course, recognize the many elements of storytelling by which they present themselves. Successful managers are usually adept at managing their own reputations. They know how to manage symbols for that purpose. The self-serving character of managerial symbol manipulation is easily seen as unattractive, and few would want to legitimize the self-aggrandizement and self-delusion that are its corollaries. Nor would many observers welcome an unconditional enthusiasm for using symbols to sustain the existing social order against all counterclaims. Critics of the establishment cannot be expected to embrace symbolic performances that have as their main consequence the reinforcement of an unacceptable social system.

These reasonable concerns about symbol manipulation are reminders of its administrative importance. Life is not just choice. It is also poetry. We live by the interpretations we make, becoming better or worse through the meanings we impute to events and institutions. Our lives change when our beliefs change. Administrators manage the way the sentiments, expectations, commitments, and faiths of individuals concerned with the organization fit into a structure of social beliefs about organizational life. Administrative theory probably underestimates the significance of this belief structure for effective organizations. As a result, it probably underestimates the extent to which the management of symbols is a part of effective administration. If we want to identify one single way in which administrators can affect organizations, it is through their effect on the world views that surround organizational life; and those effects are managed through attention to the ritual and symbolic characteristics of organizations and their administration. Whether we wish to sustain the system or change it, management is a way of making a symbolic statement.

Round theories and flat experience

In general, these observations are not particularly surprising. In most ways, they are familiar to our experience. They are less familiar, however, to the way we talk about administration. I have tried to list four emphases of administrative theory that seem to be relatively distant from our observations and experience:

First, the theoretical emphasis on change as produced by heroic leader action and the consequent emphasis on effectiveness (goal-oriented action) rather than efficiency (goal-free actions), on *leadership* rather than *management*. The theoretical rhetoric of change seems antithetical to routine, but I have argued that effective systems of routine behavior are the primary bases of organizational adaptation to an environment.

Second, the theoretical emphasis on problem solving of a classical sort in which alternatives are assessed in terms of their consequences for prior goals that are stable, precise, and exogenous. I have argued that many situations in administration involve goals that are (and ought to be) ambiguous.

Third, the theoretical emphasis on explaining variations in organizational outcomes is due to variations in top leadership skills and commitment. I have argued that when an organizational system is working well, variations in outcomes will be due largely to variables unrelated to variations in attributes of top leaders. Where top leadership affects variation in outcomes, the system is probably not functioning well.

Fourth, the theoretical emphasis on administrative action as instrumental, as being justified by the way it produces substantive consequences for important outcomes. I have argued that much of administration is symbolic, a way of interpreting organizational life in a way that allows individuals in organizations to fit their experience to their visions of human existence. Administrative processes are sacred rituals at least as much as they are instrumental acts.

If informed opinion says the earth is round but we experience it as flat, we are in danger of having to choose between our senses and our intellect. If we can, we want to discover behavior that is sensible but at the same time confirms our conventional probity — in the face of their apparent inconsistency. The usual procedure, of course, is to talk about a round world and use a flat map. In the case of the map and the earth, we are confident enough of the round theory to be willing to make a fairly precise rationalization of the map. In other cases, the issues are in greater doubt. If you experience planning as something you rarely do yet all the people you admire report that it is important, you might plausibly come to echo their comments without a clear understanding of why you talk about planning so much yet do it so little.

Like a person contemplating a naked emperor amidst courtiers exclaiming over the royal clothing, an administrator must simultaneously act intelligently and sustain a reputation for intelligence. Since theories of administration — and the talk that they generate — are part of the basis for reputation, their distance from ordinary administrative experience poses a problem. For most administrators, the difficulties are not likely to be seen as stemming from failures in administrative theory. For what I have called "administrative theory" is not some set of esoteric axioms propagated by a few high priests of academe. Rather, it is an elaboration of very general cultural beliefs about organizations, change, leadership, and administration. Most reasonable people accept them with as much confidence as they accept the notion that the earth is round, even while at the same time finding them inconsistent with important parts of organizational life.

The argument is not that administrative theory and administrative life should coincide. In general, they should not. The criterion for a good normative theory is not its descriptive accuracy. It is not necessary that the theory be correct, consistent, or even meaningful in conventional terms. It is not necessary that the theory resolve all the difficult trade-offs that impinge on administrative life. In most human domains, we maintain the maxims of a good life by violating them judiciously without claims of virtue; and we pursue goals we would not want to achieve in hopes thereby of becoming better than we are. For our theories of administration to be useful in administrative life, we require that *pursuing* (without necessarily fulfilling) the precepts of the theory improves organizations and administration. In such a spirit, administrators may struggle to follow the precepts of administrative thought, even though they are impossible, inconsistent, or unwise. Intelligent administrators might well do such a thing in full consciousness, not in hopes of fulfilling the precepts — for they would not want to do that — but in hopes of acting in a better way than they would without the struggle.

Much of standard administrative theory, including parts that have long been criticized by behavioral students of organizations, seems to me to meet such criteria. There are numerous elementary — but vital — rules of thumb that help improve the management of an organization when applied with intelligence, even though they seem either trivial or contradictory. For example, the dictum that managers should minimize the span of control *and* minimize the number of levels in the organization is obviously nonsensical as a statement of an optimization problem. It is, however, not foolish as a statement of contradictory complications in organizing. Many of the things that ancient texts on administration say seem to me similarly sensible — but not all of them. The fact that administrative theory, like a moral code, does not have to be *prima facie* sensible in order to be useful should not lead us to assume immediately that incomplete, inconsistent, or incorrect maxims are *necessarily* helpful.

Sometimes our assumptions are wrong, and the worlds we experience as flat actually are, if not entirely flat, not entirely round either. Administrators who feel that their experience with the way organizations change, with ambiguity in objectives and experience, with management incentives and careers, and with symbolic action are consistent with the kinds of research observations I have noted may well want to question conventional administrative thought and welcome alternative formulations. If these research observations capture a part of organizational truth, some of the apparently strange things that an administrator does are probably more sensible than administrative theory recognizes, and the struggle to fulfill the expectations of administrative virtue my result in actions that are less intelligent than they would have been in the absence of administrative dogma. Sometimes our theories are misleading, and the way we talk confuses the way we act.

Bibliography*

Cohen, Michael D., and March, James G. *Leadership and Ambiguity: The American College President.* New York: McGraw-Hill, 1974.

Cohen, Michael D.; March, James G.; and Olsen, Johan P. "A Garbage Can Model of Organizational Choice." *Administrative Science Quarterly* 17 (1972): 1-25.

Feldman, Martha S., and March, James G. "Information in Organizations as Signal and Symbol." *Administrative Science Quarterly,* June, 1981.

March, James C., and March, James G. "Almost Random Careers: The Wisconsin School Superintendency, 1940-1972." *Administrative Science Quarterly* 22 (1977): 377-410.

March, James C., and March, James G. "Performance Sampling in Social Matches." *Administrative Science Quarterly* 23 (1978): 434-453.

March, James G. "American Public School Administration: A Short Analysis." *School Review* 86 (1978): 217-250.

March, James G. "Bounded Rationality, Ambiguity, and the Engineering of Choice." *Bell Journal of Economics* 9 (1978): 587-608.

March, James G. "Education and the Pursuit of Optimism." *Texas Tech Journal of Education* 2 (1975): 5-17.

March, James G. "Executive Decision Making: Some Implications for Executive Compensation." In *Executive Compensation in the 1980s,* edited by David J. MacLaughlin. San Francisco: Pentacle Press, 1980.

---

* This is far from a complete bibliography. It lists only pieces to which I have contributed and is intended simply to provide a guide to a somewhat more extensive discussion of some of the issues raised here. Several of these papers have more extensive bibliographies that should be consulted for a more comprehensive, not to mention more balanced, viewpoint.

March, James G. "Footnotes to Organizational Change." Unpublished manuscript, 1980.

March, James G., "Model Bias in Social Action." *Review of Educational Research* 42 (1973): 413-429.

March, James G. "Organizational Decision Making and Theories of Choice." In *Assessing Organizational Design and Performance,* edited by Andrew Van de Ven and William Joyce. New York: Wiley Interscience, forthcoming.

March, James G. "Science, Politics and Mrs. Gruenberg." In *The National Research Council in 1979.* Washington: National Academy of Sciences, 1979.

March, James G., and Olsen, Johan P. *Ambiguity and Choice in Organizations.* Bergen: Universitetsforlaget, 1976.

Responses, Questions, and Discussion

John E. Cribbet, Chancellor at Urbana-Champaign: Dr. March, we certainly thank you for a most interesting talk. There are several memorable phrases in the speech which I am sure we shall remember from time to time. I particularly like the "madly mucking about" bit, but I suppose, to stick to a prime analogy in your speech, that the next portion of the program might really be called John Cribbet and his three light bulbs. You can judge the degree of brightness or dimness of the group as we proceed through the panel discussion. To comment on the talk, we have three individuals who will take a look at the speech from varying perspectives. First, we have a president of a university, then we have a dean of a college, and finally we have a man at the apex, a professor. Each will look at the problems from his particular viewpoint. I'm not going to make introductions. I think all of you know Dr. Ikenberry. If you don't, you don't belong in the room. I think most of you also know Dean Burnett of our College of Education, and Lou Pondy, professor in the College of Commerce and Business Administration. We shall turn first to Dr. Ikenberry's comments.

Response by Stanley O. Ikenberry

President, University of Illinois

I should entitle my remarks "A Commentary on the Hole in the Apple from the Perspective of the Worm." "How We Talk and How We Act," the title of your address, struck me as interesting. I reflected on my amazement this past year in how much of my time I have spent doing the former and how little the latter.

The theory of administration is, I suppose, like the theory of the marketplace, a philosophy of life, or the theory of many other things. For those involved in the practice of administration and involved in living and working in complex organizations, we seldom pause to think that indeed there may be a theory that would help explain certain of the frustrations that surround us each day. One of your great gifts — not only to those in colleges and universities, but in complex organizations of all kinds — is to cause us to broaden our horizons and to become sensitive to the fact that indeed there may be a more rational explanation to our lives than perhaps we had earlier perceived.

I took your earlier comments, as you reviewed certain of the conventional canons of administration, not to be outright rejection of those canons, but rather to represent an effort to go beyond them. This is the great contribution of your writing and is the stimulus that your comments give. Organizations indeed do resist change; they are *designed* to resist change in order to provide stability of operation from day to day in the way human beings relate to each other. That organizations resist change, that leadership does make a difference, that organizations tend to do better when they have a sense of purpose, that the end result does count — these four canons, it seems to me, do retain some thread of validity.

You help us to understand the complexities of modern organizational life. The fact that the external environment may be one of the more potent influences on an organization and on leadership is, I think, very well illustrated by the past two or three decades in higher education. One reflects on Dr. Henry's career as president of the University of Illinois in terms of the growth and expansion of this University. In the foreseeable future, there will not be a comparable period of growth and expansion. This growth and expansion, I dare say, Dr. Henry, was not brought about by any personal desire or drive on your part, but rather was brought about by a set of environmental forces. Had you set out to resist them, you would have run into serious problems. The challenge was neither to create change nor to resist it, but to help the University adapt and respond.

Your statement that much of administration is filled with rather unimportant and inconsequential events, Professor March, I found terribly disturbing in your comments, and I have no idea what you are talking about! When I recovered from personal offense, I stopped to think that the way a computer functions is not to achieve a single, grand solution. It solves complex problems by making repeated, minute comparisons. To a certain extent, the art of administration is a series of many small, discrete comparisons and decisions — any of which appears to be insignificant — and yet, when taken in the aggregate, eventually takes on broader significance.

To be able to live with ambiguity and to be able to comprehend it is one of the talents of administration. And for you, sir, as a theorist of administration, to articulate that principle does a great service for all of us.

Your caution against overly precise evaluation of administrative behavior is absolutely correct, and I intend to review this with the Board of Trustees at the next meeting! You are correct, too, as you remove some of the mythology from administration and place the "great person" theory into perspective. I particularly liked your concept of density, or depth of administrative talent, as being a more satisfactory explanation for the quality of organizational performance. In case you want documentation or a footnote to your text, we have had one of the best years in our history, and we did so while having a president who did not know his way to the office, an acting chancellor, an acting vice-chancellor for academic affairs, an acting vice-chancellor of research, an acting dean for the College of Liberal Arts and Sciences, an acting dean of the College of Education, a new dean of the College of Communications, and so forth. That the University of Illinois should be able to survive, in spite of the Cribbets and the Ikenberrys and the Burnetts and others, is a case in point to document your position.

I conclude with a question. I ask: Do leaders lead? Do they lead in the sense of influencing change, strengthening the sense of organizational identity, in terms of helping the organization gain a collective sense of reality, grasping a sense of common purpose — ambiguous though it may be, embracing a set of values — as tenuous as these may be, and achieving a sense of well-being — as uneasy as it may be? Do leaders lead in that sense, and if so, how do they do it within the context of your conceptual framework?

Response by Joe R. Burnett

Dean, College of Education
University of Illinois at Urbana-Champaign

I wish to talk about a number of general emphases which seem to me to pervade Professor March's paper and his and Michael D. Cohen's important volume, *Leadership and Ambiguity*.[1]

First, I am concerned about the emphasis placed upon normal change, of the dynamic stability which persists so long — among other things — the ubiquitous managers *are* average to above-average managers. I am interested about this emphasis because it invites the inference that crises do not genuinely count as such. I refer to crises of both internal and external origins. (I mean by a "crisis" a situation in which all or almost all knowledgeable, involved people will agree that there is imminent the destruction of a desirable organizational system or subsystem unless profound intervention occurs from some source.) Equally, another inference which seems invited is that there are seldom, if ever, those golden moments of a great opportunity when management can, so to speak, deliberately and dramatically change the course of history. True, we perhaps have to scale down concepts of crises and profound opportunities when talking about such prosaic things as colleges and universities, but I dare say that the economic and demographic conditions which are facing many small colleges (especially) and some large universities are prime sources of genuine crises and carry attendant, seemingly permanent, destruction of some worthy institutions. I think the response which is suggested by Professor March's work would be that *if anything could be done,* it would be done *via* normal processes of change — coping. But I think this surely begs the question with respect to crises and great opportu-

---
[1] New York: McGraw-Hill, 1974.

nities as they are experienced. At the very least, it introduces a counterfactual argument which can be neither supported nor rejected unambiguously.

Tied to this observation is Professor March's distrust of notions of the heroic leader, the "great man" theory, together with a distrust of the corollary notion of power as a prime factor in organizational analysis.[2] One senses that he disdains the notion of human reason, effort, and power as sources of significant intervention to meet a crisis or grasp the great opportunity. Yet, as I read him, he does permit the efficacy of these in exceptional cases of persons, problems, and contexts. But, if this be so, why cannot the factors be seen functioning importantly all along? Power does not have to be exceptionally dramatic in order to be power. One can find cause for rejecting the unilateral theories of great or heroic persons without relegating to unwarranted triviality the notion that some administrators have exceptional power, and sometimes they use it decisively to interfere with normal operations during both normal and abnormal (e.g., crisis) times.

Again, perhaps it is the seemingly prosaic character of college and university life — or life at the specific institutions which Professor March studied — that causes power to seem such a relatively useless concept.

There seems to be a paradox in Professor March's discussion of power. It is not a significant factor in casual analysis, yet the symbolism of power *is* important. I think it is not enough to say it is important because it makes the person who possesses the symbols feel important. That may be true. *Mere* symbolism does exist; but it would not be true for long were it not the case that symbolism was a token for *the fact of power exercised,* upon some past occasion, that potentially could be exercised again. The symbolism is a reminder and a harbinger. It has potency to signify a *real* possibility.

Let me conclude with one final observation. There are two major views of institutional and social change in the regard that I have been discussing them. One holds that change is continuous — the past is always very much like the present, the immediate future will be very much like the present. This was the view of William Graham Sumner and of Vilfredo Pareto. It was the view of Harry Truman, who said that "the only thing new in the world is the history that we don't know." I think this is Professor March's view. It lends itself to conservatism and bare meliorism. Profound change is at best a psychological response: underlying reality changes little. Folkways and mores persist and dominate.

---

[2] Ibid., pp. 197-99.

The other view is that change is importantly saltatory. In the extreme, it is the view that "the only thing one can learn from history is that one can't learn from history" (Gustav Mueller said this, I believe.) Change involves leaps, gaps, discontinuities; these are opportune moments for leadership and power by human agents. This was Marx's view and that of Gunnar Myrdal — with the latter's notion of opinion explosions and human engineering.

It may be no comfort, but both views seem essentially subjective and unverifiable or falsifiable, even in principle. This suggests that a science of organizational change is impossible. Perhaps organizational theory is at best heavily an art, an "aesthetic" (as Santayana called all of life). Certainly Professor March's views represent a high expression, and a worthy one, in this dimension.

I am honored to have had the chance to respond to — and perhaps provoke — Professor March.

Response by Louis R. Pondy

Professor, College of Commerce and Business Administration
University of Illinois at Urbana-Champaign

Let me pose a question at the outset that I hope to answer by the end of my comments: Can we afford to take Jim March's view of administration seriously? That is a different question from asking whether he's right, or whether we *should* take him seriously.

March's paper might be viewed as an aberration if measured against the conventional wisdom of administrative practice, but if you set it in a different context, it seems quite sensible. I think that we can best understand the paper within the historic stream of debate, over a variety of issues, that has been going on in administrative theory for the past forty years. The paper can also be seen as an extension of Jim March's own work over the past twenty-five years. That debate is over the actuality, the possibility, the desirability of rational administrative action. In one view, administrative action is directed and motivated by the deliberate pursuit of stated goals and objectives; in the counterview, administrative action muddles along, activated only by the random processes of local adaptation.

The list of people who have participated in the debate includes scholars such as Chester Barnard, who in the late 1930s described organizations as rational, cooperative decision systems, and Herbert Simon, who first during the 1940s (and later as March's collaborator) tried to rescue rationality by inventing the concept of limited rationality, but intended rationality, nonetheless. During the 1950s, Charles Lindblom propounded his concept of incremental decision making (March and Lindblom were both at Yale at the same time, March as a student and Lindblom as a faculty member, and Jim's own views of decision making reflect the Lindblomian incrementalism). During the 1960s, James D. Thompson described organizations as being faced with the dilemma of simultaneously operating a closed rational system in the short run and an open adaptive system in the long run. March's own work with Dick Cyert in the early 1960s, on the behavioral theory of the firm, is part of the same debate where decision making was seen as characterized not only by limited rationality but also by political behavior and the quasi-resolution of conflict. And in the decade just past, the random, nonrational side of the debate has been reinforced by scholars such as Henry Mintzberg, who — as a result of intensive studies of the daily life of managers — characterized administrative action as brief, fragmented, interrupted, and more like Brownian motion than directed action. There have been others who have weighed in on the "nonrational" side of the debate as well. Chris Argyris and Donald Schoen, in particular, have observed the distinction between "espoused theory" and "theory-in-action" and have argued in contrast to Professor March that the two should be coincident.

Let me try to sharpen this ongoing debate. I'd like to argue that the key word in the title of Professor March's talk is the word *and*. It's noteworthy that he did not title the paper "How We Talk *vs.* How We Act," or "How We Talk *Coincident with* How We Act," but "How We Talk *and* How We Act." That is, he tends to see action and talk as two separate domains of discourse, delicately coupled: where *talk* is informed by a concept of rational motivation, of rational pursuit, of progress towards some ideal end, *talk* as rationalization, justification and the creation of legitimacy, *talk* as the province of the top level of administration in complex organizations, what he also described as the "level of interpretation"; but where *action* is informed not by global rationality, but by local adaptation, with aggregate action resulting from the sum of disaggregated adaptations, not leading toward any specific ideal, but participating in an evolutionary drift, where "goals" follow *actions* as retrospective justifications, rather than as pre-set objectives.

In sum, March comes down on the nonrational side of the administrative rationality debate. There is a place for rational discourse in his model, but it is relegated to top-level administrative talk, which, he argues, is mostly *decoupled* from the real action in the infrastructure of the organization.

Now that we have placed March's views in a historical context, let me discuss some implications of his model by examining the different ways in which malfunctions manifest themselves within March's view and according to the conventional wisdom. In the latter case, administrative failure results in action not following talk closely enough, but within the Marchian view, there are several counterintuitive ways in which organizations can go wrong. One type of malfunction results from attempting to make *action consistent with talk,* that is, by interfering with the processes of local adaptation in the name of obedience to rational discourse. I attended a very interesting lecture recently on the use of student credit hours as a kind of doctrine, or mythology, for administrative action — in particular as the basis for the internal allocation of resources at this and other universities. The very sage point was made that the concept of student credit hours was a useful device for communicating with external agencies, especially the state legislature, for the purpose of picturing the university as a productive educational institution; but that the university errs by taking the student credit hour concept too seriously and actually basing decisions — especially budget decisions — upon it, thereby setting in motion strategies by subunits to out-game the system. March's argument would be that we ought to talk one way about student credit hours for external consumption, and then make our internal allocation decisions on more sensible grounds that are not subject to tactics of beating the system.

A second way in which organizations can go wrong is by making *talk consistent with action,* that is, by freezing possible futures into the mold of the present and, perhaps, undermining the environmental legitimacy that is so necessarily provided by talk produced for external consumption.

A third malfunction is single-minded reliance on the "great leader." Lester Seligman has observed that the presidential debates create a serious dysfunction by focusing attention away from the parties and toward the personalities of individual candidates. What we really need, in March's view, is to get a routine administrative apparatus into place that will produce the desired actions. Falling back on the "great leader" myth directs our attention away from the task of building a workable administrative apparatus that facilitates local adaptation.

I'm in basic agreement with much of what March says (probably because I was a student of his twenty years ago!). However, I do see some problems with his analysis. He has left completely unspecified who has the responsibility for creating the routine procedures that normalize the process of change. One possibility is that the routine procedures themselves evolve through a process of local adaptations, but this is left unsaid. In my judgment, March also overstates the homogenizing effects of the selection process. He bases his analysis on the unspoken assumption that the sequenced selection filters all on the same set of criteria. If the selection criteria change from level to level, then it is more likely than March suggests that incompetent administrators will make it through the selection processes to the top. A related problem is that the criteria that are applied during selection are not necessarily those criteria that are appropriate for good action once in office. There's no guarantee that I can see anywhere in his system that the selection procedures would, in fact, produce people of uniform but high competence. But then, in March's theory, administrators don't affect action anyway, so what does it matter if they are incompetent?

I was troubled, as was Dean Burnett, about the difficulty of explaining revolutionary change within his system. He seems to argue, as does Thomas Kuhn, about the structure of scientific revolutions — that revolutionary change can arise from the gradual accumulation of minor anomalies. March suggests that dramatic events are produced not by dramatic causes but by routine, elementary processes. This is very much a Kuhnian view of change.

Finally, I believe that March has overstated the case that decisions made by top administrators have no impact on organizational action at the lowest levels. For example, in the University, the chancellor and vice-chancellor may not make decisions about textbooks, classroom topics, and so forth, but they do make decisions about decision makers — what I would call "second order decisions": decisions about the selection of deans, search committees, and so forth. Although those choices are once or twice removed from the level of action and though they surely are symbolic in content, just as surely, they have substantive impact on the conduct of University affairs at the lowest level — albeit through indirect means.

There were some surprises in what March said. He speaks more favorably about classical administrative principles than I had been aware of in his work before. He also seemed to make a conscious attempt to move away from decision making as a central analytical concept — a major departure considering his twenty-five-year career of research on decision making.

Despite what I view as problems in the presentation, I do think that March's theory is closer to reality than the traditional model described in his opening comments. The accuracy of his model is not at issue. What is at issue is the effect of his theory on practice, and that brings me back to my opening question: Can we afford to take March's view seriously? What he is saying is the following: Effective administration consists firstly of treating talk and action in fact as separate domains and, secondly, of maintaining *the fiction* that talk and action are consistent with one another. He has rubbed our collective noses in the truth of this functional hypocrisy. However, by exposing the hypocrisy, he risks destroying its very effectiveness. Those who take March seriously will look with skepticism on any future administrator's assertion that his or her talk and action are indeed consistent. This realization puts us in an uncomfortable and inescapable double bind. In order to preserve administrative effectiveness founded on March's doctrine of functional hypocrisy, we must keep March's theory a closely guarded secret and should immediately adjourn these proceedings! The only sensible response is to take March seriously in the privacy of our own thoughts, but to deny the truth of his thesis in public. At least that is what I would expect a truly clever and effective administrator to do.

Questions and Discussion

Chancellor Cribbet: I am not entitled to say anything except as a presiding officer. I would like to say one thing, however. I rather suspect that Jim March is correct, and I'm sorry if he is. I would have to confess that I'm a bit of a romantic. I tend to live by illusions and I don't want to have all of them destroyed. I do happen to believe in the "great person" theory of institutions, i.e., that people can move institutions. Otherwise, why do we bother to take on the burdensome administrative role?

Professor March: Rather than try to respond comprehensively to the thoughtful comments of my friends, let me restrict myself to one theme that runs through several of the speakers. The theme is an important one, and I fear that there is little I can add to what has been said by people like Ibsen, Tolstoy, Shaw, Cervantes, and Borges. But I can at least serve as a reminder of the possible relations between the prosaic concerns of management and the musings of General Kutuzov at the Battle of Borodino. It has been suggested, perhaps with some justice, that I have a less heroic view of leadership than some others do. Indeed, it has been suggested that such a view, even if correct, is pernicious — for it undermines belief in human efficacy, a vital basis for commitment on the part of the leaders. I am inclined toward a somewhat more classical view. I think that a fundamental problem of leadership, as of life, is the problem of sustaining intelligent optimism in the face of intelligent skepticism about great hopes. The serious hero is one who continues to act appropriately while understanding the limited relevance of action.

In Ibsen's *Wild Duck*, Dr. Relling argues against talking about *ideals*. He prefers the plain-speaking word *lies*. And yet, he says, we should not destroy the "life-lies" by which we understand our existence. For 'if you take the illusions away from an ordinary person, you take life as well." Like Lou Pondy, Dr. Relling suggests avoiding realism about the limits of human control over history. In a world in which it is hard to tell when, or whether, they are able to influence the course of events, we wish leaders to try to do good (even though it may be futile) rather than have them take the chance (however small) of foregoing an opportunity to make a better world. To encourage action rather than despair and withdrawal, we might embrace a myth of personal significance. As Lou Pondy suggests, we might want to ask whether we can afford the luxury of doubting the myths of management. It is a reasonable question, as one might expect, for both Dr. Relling and Dr. Pondy are reasonable people.

The question is reasonable, but I think it understates the risk, and overstates the feasibility, of fooling ourselves. In particular, life at the top of an organization provides mixed evidence for leadership significance. Although ordinary flattery and the limited imagination of organizational gossip is usually reassuring about managerial effects, direct managerial experience will often disappoint great expectations and confound the assessment of personal importance. If we require heroic action to be justified by great hopes, we invite a managerial tendency toward self-delusion or cynicism.

During my remarks, I tried to suggest one way of protecting leaders from some of the corruptions of discovering that they are not uniquely important. Suppose we consider the finals of the world championship 100-meter dash. If by some chance an average sprinter were able to sneak into the competition, we know such a person would be left far behind. We know that any world class sprinter who fails to train to the limit, or who is not committed to winning, or who slips momentarily in the race will also be left behind. But by the time you observe the world championship finals, you have the best sprinters, trained to the limit, and running their best. A consequence is that there is usually no reliable difference among them. Each is about equally likely to win. Top management is like that. Screening on the way to the top assures that chief executives will form a relatively homogeneous group. They are people who are ambitious, dedicated, able, and running as hard as they can. Like world class sprinters (or light bulbs), they will all do their best and do well. They are important, but they are substantially interchangeable. Leaders generally prefer the champion sprinter metaphor to the light bulb metaphor; but both are reminders that in a well-functioning system, hopes for personal significance should not be linked to expectations of indispensability.

Such cautions may help, but, in the end, great actions can be sustained more reliably if they are not based on great hopes for consequence. The basic text in leadership is written by Cervantes. After a series of seemingly irrational romantic actions, Don Quixote says, "No doubt you set me down in your mind as a fool and a madman, and it would be no wonder if you did, for my deeds do not argue anything else. But for all that, I would have you take notice that I am neither so mad nor so foolish as I must have seemed to you.... All knights have their special parts to play.... I, then, as it has fallen to my lot to be a member of the knight-errantry, cannot avoid attempting all that to me seems to come within the sphere of my duties." In effect, Quixote says that, of course, the world is absurd — filled with windmills, donkeys, and actions of no consequence. But it is precisely the absurdity of life that makes affirmation and action a declaration of humanity rather than merely an instrumental act. For Quixote, great actions do not depend on great expectations, but rather on a conception of how a good person lives. It is a noble and romantic sentiment, and one that I think we might commend to college presidents, corporate chief executive officers, and heads of governmental agencies — within reason.

Questioner (Anne Huff, Assistant Professor, Business Administration, UIUC): I was interested in the comment about political parties, and I wonder if Professor March could make some comment about the political system in the light of his theory. I personally am not as confident about the functioning of light bulbs in politics as in universities.

Professor March: Organizations may certainly vary in the extent to which their selection and promotion procedures produce relatively homogeneous pools of relatively competent top managers. I would think it might be possible that the present political system in the United States is a somewhat less reliable filter than the system of promotion in some hierarchical organizations. I would be cautious about overdoing the distinction, however. The primary criteria for advancement in politics are political, and I think it is plausible to argue that there is less variation in political skills among leading politicians than there is among fledgling politicians. As a result, I think it is plausible to argue that although political leaders are important for the functioning of the political system, variations in the outcomes in political systems do not much depend on which specific political leader is chosen from the pool of candidates. I am speaking, of course, not about the variations due to fluctuations in the party in power (in democratic systems), but fluctuations due to variations in political skill at the top. Those latter fluctuations seem to me likely to be more modest than reading contemporary newspapers will suggest.

Questioner (Dorothy Robinson, Elementary School Principal, Danville, Illinois, and Doctoral Candidate in Administration, Higher, and Continuing Education, UIUC): In applying some of the things you said to my daily life as an administrator, I wonder if it is perhaps not that the goals are ambiguous, but that an administrator is consciously managing conflicting expectations from subordinates, peers, superiors, and fringe groups which have political influence.

Professor March: Conflict in goals is clearly a characteristic of schools, as it is of hospitals, government agencies, and business firms. By emphasizing ambiguity in goals, I did not mean to ignore explicit conflict as a phenomenon. Good managers know how to arrange coalitions, to bargain, and to logroll agreements. I would, however, add a footnote to writings about organizations as political systems or education as a political system. Many theories of coalitions and bargaining in educational organizations overlook the extent to which the concerns of participants involved in education are embedded in their other concerns. As a result, they sometimes overlook the way in which politics is affected by factors influencing attention. Particularly in relatively minor political arenas, participants wander in and out. The resources they are willing to devote to that particular arena change. These wanderings and changes depend on the mix of concerns and opportunities in other arenas, and that mix shifts in a way that seems almost fortuitous. As a result, conflict and political bargaining do not have the kind of fine-grained stability that might be expected. Organizational managers can, of course, try to manipulate attention. They can, for example, provide symbolic issues to attract potential participants who might help them. They can time projects to coincide with a favorable mix of attention. When you recognize the ambiguities of attention in a political system, however, you may want to see the system as somewhat more "ambiguous" and somewhat less "political" than the political metaphor usually suggests.

Questioner (Professor Pondy): Anne Huff and I are doing a study of school superintendents. One of them is faced with a school closing issue in which there could have been intense conflicts between people who don't want to see the building torn down, others who don't want to see senior citizens moved in, and others who don't want to see real estate tenants moved in. One of the things he's done that has been very clever is to keep the antagonists out of snowball throwing distance of each other. What's happened recently is that a brand new potential buyer has shown up on the scene and that has resolved the problem. If he had forced a joining of the issue too soon, it would have produced intense conflict in the community. His genius was to keep things suspended in limbo long enough until an expected solution simply showed up on its own accord.

Professor March: I suspect that administrative theory may sometimes have unduly complicated life by emphasizing the benefits of participation and involvement without noting their costs.

Questioner (Professor Pondy): We had another superintendent who came into a district, developed his own program, and then tried to sell it to the entire community. But he harked back to his administrative theory courses where he read something about participative management and decided that the way to sell his program was to invite participation. So, he offered to meet with any group in the community to explain his program, wherever and whenever they wanted, and he wound up meeting for thirty-seven straight nights. What he did was to organize all the opposition against him, and the program was defeated. Again, it was the result of joining the issue too firmly, too soon, and too directly without letting it develop its own rhythm. That was a beautiful case of taking a theory of participative management too seriously.

Questioner (Hugh Petrie, Professor, Educational Policy Studies, UIUC): I appreciated your suggestion that ordinary bureaucratic procedures, appropriately carried out, are not as often recognized as being adaptive forms of behavior as they should be. On the other hand, I also have a good deal of sympathy for the point that Dean Burnett and Lou Pondy made in their comments that you either denied or at least ignored the possibility that on occasion the bureaucratic tendency, given significant changes in the ecology, will not be adaptive. I did not think your two allusions, as much as I loved both of them in your response, spoke to that issue. Are there crises where just doing the good old things well will not be sufficient to bring about the needed change?

Professor March: I think the answer to your question is clearly yes as long as you recognize that what you call "doing the good old things" will often produce notable changes and that profound changes in organizations can be produced by relatively modest interventions. That is, mundane responses of an organization to dramatic changes in the environment can be a source of radical organizational change, and carefully timed minor actions that exploit the natural processes of organizations to amplify them are a primary tool of effective leadership. With those caveats, however, I think it is important to recognize that organizations, like species, may require some kind of variation from sensible routines — some kind of foolishness. The general problem is not that organizations resist innovations and change stupidly, although that certainly occurs at times. The more general problem stems from the fact that most proposed changes are bad ideas. If you take a proposed change at random, it will have a negative expected value. That doesn't mean there are no good ideas. In fact, some possible changes are very, very good ideas. Unfortunately, it is hard to tell the good ones from the bad ones; and, on the average, an organization will be hurt by being the first to try a new direction. As a result, it is ordinarily not sensible for any organization to make a change until some other organization has done so successfully. In short, resistance to change in organizations is typically not a sign of rigidity or stupidity but a generally sensible strategy. The problem for the larger system of organizations is to induce individual organizations to make enough dumb changes to ensure that the dumb things that actually turn out to be useful are discovered. This is probably not the place to identify the various ways in which organizations are made foolish in order to help the system of organizations, but it might be appropriate to mention the special role of foolishness in management. One of the ways in which innovation is produced is by encouraging managers to "make their marks." Most role descriptions of management put a premium on doing something. On the average, organizations are probably hurt more than helped by their own managerial initiatives; but the system of organizations profits from these foolish experiments with change. A small fraction of the dumb things that are done turn out to be very smart indeed. By emphasizing the importance of managerial action, organizations lead ambitious managers to do things that are not in the best interest of their own organizations but are a form of altruism extended toward the wider system.

Questioner (Dean Joe Burnett): Many people would thoroughly enjoy and learn from the final section of Professor March's volume on tactics of administrative leadership. These are, I think, very instructive. I wanted to ask one question. What would you say Lee Iacocca's role was in the management of the Chrysler crisis recently? Was that a straight line development of ordinary managerial routine, or was that crisis intervention?

Professor March: I think it's a good question, but I don't have any basis for an answer.

Questioner (Fred Coombs, Associate Professor, Educational Policy Studies, UIUC): I'm not sure that you had an opportunity to respond to Pondy's invitation to spell out some of the mechanisms by which organizations adapt. It seems to some of us who haven't studied them as closely as you that at times organizations adapt very nicely to changes in the external environment, but that at other times one can identify quite dysfunctional things going on in the organization. I presume the "inspiration of foolishness" is one way in which they may adapt, but are there other mechanisms?

Professor March: I think it may be appropriate to distinguish change from adaptation. Change is probably necessary to adaptation, but not all change is adaptive. My basic argument is that change occurs routinely in organizations through some simple processes. I think of such ordinary processes as problem solving, learning, selection, imitation, rule following, conflict management, and turnover. These processes are powerful adaptive mechanisms. Most of the time they allow an organization to function effectively in its environment, changing as the world changes. However, the same processes that produce adaptive change will sometimes lead to maladaptive change. Selection can lead to over-specialization, learning can lead to superstitious learning, problem solving can lead to incentives for gaming, and so on. At the same time, there are requirements for changes that are maladaptive in the short run but needed in the long run. Managerial foolishness is one way in which such things are introduced. Organizational slack is another. Ambiguity and loose coupling are others.

Questioner (William Staerkel, President, Parkland College): There are also other things that produce change among which are the pressures and forces of the outside environment. For example, in 1957 Sputnik was launched, and as a nation we fumbled around for awhile. Then *Life* magazine, among others, suddenly decided that the schools were at fault, and that we weren't teaching enough science. So all the schools began to increase their science offerings, and as a superintendent of schools, you were a helpless captive. If you wanted to survive, you had to be a proponent of science emphasis in the schools. The same thing is occasionally true of foreign languages. There are times when they become fashionable in the elementary schools, and, when this occurs, if you're in a wealthy suburb such as Palo Alto, you will find that the superintendent had better be for teaching foreign languages in elementary schools. I especially appreciated your theory of administration because it gives an administrator tremendous opportunity to do what he wants to do, or feels that he should do, and not be concerned about being wrong or inconsistent with established administrative principles. Personally, I believe that a successful administrator really has to function in that way. That's my own belief. There's the story of the college president standing on the corner of the street visiting with a friend, when a big crowd of people is noted walking down the other side of the street. The president says to the friend, "I have to go with these people." His friend asks, "Who are they?" He replies, "They're my faculty. I don't know where they're going, but I'm their leader and I have to get in front of them." Now, does that typify your idea of the power of an organization and the function of a college president?

Professor March: If I said anything to suggest that external pressures and imitation are not important in organizational change, I certainly misspoke. The epidemiology of innovation in organizations is not unlike the epidemiology of measles among a group of school children, and we cannot observe organizational change without being impressed by the extent to which ideas (both good and bad) spread among organizations. Each individual manager, of course, is able to see the catching of the disease in terms of choice and managerial action; but an observer might be pardoned for taking a somewhat more epidemiological perspective.

As far as the college president who watches where the faculty is going and hurries to lead them, I think it is a good vision because it reveals the ambiguity of leadership in at least two important ways. The first is the old maxim that leadership requires followership. If a faculty is going firmly in a particular direction, a president can probably be most useful by running to get in front of them with the kind of openness about objectives that allows discovery of new ones. The second feature of the story is perhaps less obvious. There is rarely *a* faculty in a college or university. Different parts of a faculty run in different directions, and some parts run in several directions at the same time. One of the options of leadership is the option of announcing (within limits) which of these directions is the one in which "the faculty" is moving.

Questioner (Thomas J. Sergiovanni, Professor and Chairman, Administration, Higher, and Continuing Education): I'd like for you to comment on the cultural aspects of leadership. I know you gave some attention to this issue in your paper but probably not enough. Consider President Staerkel's comments about the president having to get out in front of the faculty once it decides to move, for example. It would seem to me, Jim, that one key leverage point an administrator has — be he or she a chairperson, dean, or president — is the ability to improve (maintain, nurture, alter) the culture of the organization. Chancellor Cribbet and other administrators at the University of Illinois pretty much let the faculty go and try to catch up with them later. If, as administrators, they do a good job of building and nurturing images of what this University is about, of setting standards and socializing people to a particular ethic, they can have confidence that when they finally do get in front, the faculty will be running off in a decent direction — wherever the ending, it will be a happy one. Would you elaborate on your comments referring to the more symbolic and interpretive aspects of teaching?

Professor March: I might add three general things about cultures, or world views, or whatever else we want to call these broad sets of beliefs and practices that permeate our lives. First, no administrator can control them arbitrarily. There are many other forces impinging on beliefs, and the marginal control that any one person has over them is ordinarily small. Second, exercising influence over the culture of an organization is not a route to precise managerial control. You do not control the adoption or implementation of specific policies. Rather, you affect a climate for possible policies. On the whole, I think that is a better vision; but it is a perspective different from those that emphasize fine-grained control over organizational outcomes. Third, the development of organizational world views is more than an instrument of policy. It is important in its own right. We live by the poetry of life, and if an administrator helps to provide an interpretation of life that elaborates our lives in interesting ways, we are enriched. Administrators are poets. They help us experience events and actions in ways that make life more meaningful. But Lou Pondy is the real expert on this subject. Do you want to add anything Lou?

Questioner (Professor Pondy): Just that I agree very strongly. I published a paper two years ago called "Beyond Open System Models of Organization" which was a critique of the reigning theoretical book in the field of organizational sociology, which treated organizations as though they were machines and managers as though they were machine operators. If you buy into the machine metaphor, that's a sensible way of thinking about administration. If you present administrators with the machine metaphor directly, they'll doubtless deny it. But if you listen to the fragments of their language, you get a much more accurate understanding of what metaphor is implicitly in use. For example, administrators talk about the "output" of the university. The culture metaphor is really a different kind of metaphor. It pictures the institution as a language-using community, a sense-making community — one which has a history in which myths and stories are taken seriously, in which people aren't thought of as replaceable parts. Within the culture metaphor, the function of the administrator as poet, as linguist, as mythmaker, makes more sense than as machine operator.

Questioner (Daniel Alpert, Director of the Center for Advanced Study and Professor of Physics, UIUC): I found many of your comments to ring very true to my experience with a university as an organized anarchy. On the other hand, I found a different feeling of the role of management in certain other kinds of organizations. For example, in comprehensive R & D laboratories some turn out many new inventions, new technologies — others just don't, even though their people have similar backgrounds and credentials. Maybe it's like the difference between the demands on the management of a track team and the management of a football team. Perhaps it's that, but I do sense that there are significant differences — whether or not the management of such a collective enterprise has a theory for how it's doing. I wonder if you'd comment.

Professor March: As you know, Dan, research on R & D management is a hot topic these days. I suspect you are right — that managing an

R & D laboratory is different from managing a university, which is different from managing a business firm. Nevertheless, I think that most of what I said applies to each of them. Consider, for example, my comments about precision in management. We generally note that some organizations have clearer goals than others, and that is important to understanding how they function. But the observation that precisely measured objectives lead to the management of accounts (and thus to costs as well as benefits) probably applies to a wide variety of organizations. Rational R & D managers, like rational business firm executives and rational college presidents, will recognize that they can often control their accounts more easily than they can control their organizations. So, they will spend time trying to discover ways to "score" well without necessarily "doing" well. In the R & D management case, if you evaluate managers by the number of patentable inventions their organizations make (per engineer), you will stimulate some managerial imagination about how to increase that statistic without changing what is happening in the laboratory.

Questioner (President Ikenberry): I guess I have one. That is, having listened both to the paper and listened to our discussion, I found your theory to be increasingly useful in terms of explaining the norm — that is let us say 90 to 95 percent of the variance — but yet not so helpful in explaining the other 5 to 10 percent of the variance. Going back to a couple of the illustrations you used earlier, I then have asked myself, "Well, isn't life fought on the margin anyway?" And isn't it the task of an organization to try to go beyond the 90 percent to begin to cope with the other 5 or 10 percent which basically spells the difference, for example, between a Stanford and an "X"? That difference between Stanford and "X" or Illinois and "X" is, in fact, what the enterprise is all about. Do you grasp my frustration? I would be interested in your comment.

Professor March: I think there is a lot of truth in what you say, but I want to turn it around a bit. Sometimes it is tempting to define the task of theory as maximizing the explained variance in the phenomena we observe, but that is a potentially misleading perspective. In fact, a good deal of the variance in many situations can be explained from ordinary knowledge. Although ordinary knowledge is sometimes wrong and frequently uncodified, there is little point in constructing theories that are heavily redundant with what is well established in ordinary knowledge. What a theory should do is to contribute at the margin to what we know, to maximize the joint product of ordinary knowledge and theoretical knowledge. This means that much of the time a good theory will focus on the things that are easily forgotten by people who are in the field, or things that people know but don't understand. If in this joint endeavor we someday manage to understand 90 percent of what is going on, I'd be delighted. I doubt that we are there yet, at least in understanding organizations. But wherever we are in absolute terms, you are quite right: the game is played at the margin. Where we might differ, although I am not sure that we would, is in whether the explanation of the last 10 percent is more likely to be found by introducing new variables (e.g., power, personality, culture, administrative skill) or by understanding better the ways in which the ordinary processes we think we understand so well sometimes produce unusual outcomes. Given where we are now, I think the latter task is one that should command a fair share of our attention in trying to develop our theories of organizations and management.

Hanna Holborn Gray, president of the University of Chicago, is uniquely qualified to speak about liberal arts education in the U.S. Dr. Gray is an historian whose special interests include humanism, political and historical thought, and politics in the Renaissance and the Reformation. Born in Heidelberg, Germany, she received her bachelor of arts degree from Bryn Mawr College in 1950 and her Ph.D. in history from Harvard University in 1957. From 1950 to 1952, she was a Fulbright Scholar at Oxford University.

Dr. Gray was on the faculties of Bryn Mawr College, Harvard University, Northwestern University, Yale University and Oxford University before being named to her present position in 1978. She is a fellow of the American Academy of Arts and Sciences and a member of the American Philosophical Society and the National Academy of Education. She is a trustee of the National Humanities Center, Andrew W. Mellon Foundation, Howard Hughes Foundation and the Center for Advanced Study in the Behavioral Sciences. She has received honorary degrees from more than forty major colleges and universities, including Princeton, Columbia, Yale and Michigan.

The eighth Henry Lecture was presented Ocober 15, 1981, at the University of Illinois at Chicago Circle.

The Liberal Arts Revisited

by Hanna Holborn Gray
President
The University of Chicago

Let me begin by citing two texts with an almost scriptural connotation. The first comes from Alexis de Tocqueville writing in his *Democracy in America* about what he saw as characteristic of American culture, of American attitudes and approaches toward matters intellectual. He was concerned that there was too pronounced or exclusive a bias in American culture toward the practical, or technical, applications of learning at the expense of basic knowledge. In this connection, he observed, "If the light by which we are guided is ever extinguished, it will dwindle by degrees and expire of itself. By dint of close adherence to more applications, principles would be lost sight of, and when the principles were wholly forgotten, the methods could no longer be invented and men would continue without intelligence and without art to apply scientific processes no longer understood."

The second text comes from another major commentator on the American scene, Charles Dillon Stengel, also known as Casey, who said about a pitcher on his team, "He has wonderful stuff and wonderful control, and throws strikes, which shows he is educated. But then say you're educated, and you can't throw strikes, then they don't leave you in too long."

Both passages reveal something of the tension, something of the issues that have always dominated the debates in our own society over what education is about and what education is for. That is the tension that arises from what one might call an instrumental, or utilitarian, conception of education as having to do with application rather than the search for the principles of knowledge. This view holds that the justification of education in a free society has to do ultimately with the tests of citizenship, of public service, with the criteria of whether education can be translated into professional and vocational goals. It has also to do with the question as to whether education in fact fits people for those needs. That, too, has reflected a long-standing conflict in our thinking about education.

Mark Twain once said that he had never let his schooling interfere with his education. There is a long history to the notion that the school of hard knocks, the world, experience *per se*, must be the true teachers as opposed to any school — that formal schooling may in fact corrupt and dilute one's learning powers, make one not only unfit for some real world, for some vocation, but in effect make it more difficult to undergo that genuine education which is derived from experience.

Now these kinds of differing and contrasting views about what education is about and what education is for, and what the larger social and the particular individual purposes to be realized through education might be, are characteristic not just of thinking about education in America (whatever may be our own special emphasis), but they are constants in educational thinking over the centuries. Because to think about education beyond discussing a particular curriculum or syllabus, or trying to describe what requirements people should have to qualify for college, or what they should study when in college — to think about education in terms of its purpose and its basic substance is, in fact, to be thinking about a great deal more. It is, in essence, a way in which people frame what might be called their ideal human types: what kind of person, what kind of competence, what kinds of goals might ideally characterize a society and its inhabitants and how they should be educated toward *becoming* such individuals possessing such competence and directed toward a set of common goals.

Therefore, it is not surprising that the great works of educational philosophy have been written by utopians and quasi-utopians: the Thomas Mores, Platos, Rousseaus, and others who asked themselves how might we create an ideal society, an ideal human being. In putting those questions, the utopian or quasi-utopian authors (for it's not at all clear, for example, that More was really a utopian) were in effect inquiring "What role can education have in producing such a society, in shaping such people?"

At some point, the values that we assert as those by which we guide life in the present must be values that we attempt to achieve, and to further for succeeding generations, through education. And yet, on the other side, combined with the utopian impulse there is the impulse to use such models of ideal education, or the educational enterprise, as a way of criticizing the present, of looking at what is deficient — not only in contemporary education but in contemporary ethics and government — in the manners and conduct of a world which may be condemned as corrupt and which its critics would wish to see measure up to some higher ideal.

That critical awareness of the deficiencies of the present and the attempt to discern the contours of the future leads inevitably to thinking about education: what education is about and what education is for. All of us, as we think about education, about its improvement, about how to design a curriculum or the requirements for a bachelor's degree, are somehow criticizing what we see as the inadequacies of the present, perhaps criticizing what we see as the weaknesses of our own education. Furthermore, all of us are in some way trying to describe or to penetrate a future, since education must be for the future. Education is, as someone once said, "the debt that we owe to future generations." We may perhaps be making wrong guesses about the future, but we are trying to decide what will be the needs and opportunities which will provide for future generations the kind of education that will lead to human competence, civic responsibility, professional ability, and individual fulfillment.

Those are not easy goals. Side by side with that set of ideals there runs also that sense of education as an instrumental activity, education as a set of training exercises that must ultimately have some practical effects.

In our own society we have presumably tried to reconcile those two traditions, sometimes to emphasize one more than the other. We have sometimes said that, more narrowly, education should lead to a particular opportunity for a given kind of work, a given kind of life. We have tended to say that the justification for the enormous resources we should pour into education has to do with the social and economic consequences of such investment. At the same time, we have also said that education ought to be desirable in and of itself. We have asserted that about the tradition of the liberal arts above all, for this lies at the heart of thinking about education in our four-year colleges and university colleges. Increasingly it is felt that the liberal arts are in trouble. If to think about the liberal arts is to reflect on educational purpose, then there is asserted in some sense a crisis of higher education more generally in our time.

The contrast typically made between liberal and vocational education expresses a kind of confusion. "Vocational" conveys the sense of a training that is narrowly directed to external goals and exclusively technical skills — not so much training the mind as teaching a person to perform a certain kind of activity. And yet the deepest meaning of vocation is very different: a calling that embodies an inner and compelling commitment. Thus we speak of a religious vocation or the vocation of a teacher, a doctor. Such a vocation may be professional in nature. We mean that one's profession is chosen out of some larger imperative and goal. It's interesting that we should have chosen to use that term to connote something confined and external rather than to express what might in fact be the outcome of liberal learning. The consequences of breadth, of liberality, of seeing professional training in a wider context would be to arouse a sense of vocation rather than to reduce young men and young women to narrow vocationalism. In that use of terminology, there is, I think, something symptomatic about the kinds of conflict and the kinds of issues that have characterized our discussions of what education is about and what education is for.

Once again these are questions that have of course been discussed in every age. In every age, the question of what ought to be the character of education has been similarly debated. Within those debates, the discussion over the liberal arts tradition has been especially acute. Through the centuries, the nature and the tradition of the liberal arts have been defined and redefined. On the one hand, there is some continuity in the essence of belief as to what the liberal arts might be about. But on the other hand, there have been extraordinary changes over the centuries, as we know, in the range and reference of the liberal arts tradition itself.

The ancients defined the liberal arts as those studies and those arts that were worthy of a *free man*. They really meant free as opposed to slave, and they really meant men as opposed to women; but, by extension, that term has been taken out of the context of an earlier civilization. We now would agree that the liberal arts are those studies worthy of free men and women in their capacity as human beings. We understand that freedom has to do not only with a state of personal and even political freedom, but with a state of informed cultural awareness, with a capacity for critical judgment, and the highest regard placed on the independence and the responsibility exercised by such critical judgment. This embraces also a state of critical moral awareness, which includes the value of intellectual integrity as a dimension of freedom.

Behind us lie centuries of debate as to how much of the liberal arts an educated person ought to know and whether a liberal arts training is really the best and most effective or even the most useful kind of education. In the period of the Renaissance (from which our modern understanding of a liberal arts education takes its origin), the humanists looked at and criticized the educational structures and assumptions of their day and saw them as revealing the larger dimensions and deficiencies of their own time.

People tend to think of the Renaissance as a period of self-conscious new beginnings. The humanists thought it possible that they might produce great reform in the world, but they also thought it possible that things had never been worse and could never be reformed. Their educational thinking was the vehicle by which they criticized the society of their own time: its ethical values, its culture. Their diagnoses were as follows, whether right or wrong. The humanists believed that the kinds of knowledge and of scholarship and of advanced education, which characterized the university system of their own day, were too academic, too narrow, too pedantic, too specialized. In short, they thought that the universities of their time offered only a professional education, an education so highly specialized that it spoke in no way to the human condition or to the realities of the world in which people needed to be educated. It had little to do, they thought, with what they saw as the overwhelming need for education and for its foundation. In their view, that had to do with the need to deal with men in their capacities as social beings, as members of society, and also in their capacities as individuals whose ethical character needed to be shaped so that they would lead better lives and in turn improve the world around them. The humanists believed that the assumptions attached to scholarship and education in their own time led away from the investigation of human nature and the human condition. They believed these led to simply abstract and, in their view, sterile forms of speculation and inquiry — such was the humanists' condemnation of metaphysics and natural philosophy of their day. They thought these had no meaning for the kinds of problems which educated lay people — people who would be citizens and politicians and businessmen — really needed to understand. Therefore, from their critique of what was wrong with contemporary thought and scholarship in the university, the humanists concluded that by contrast an education in the liberal arts was that form of learning most relevant to the development of people who would become masters of their own world and leaders toward an improved future. They thought it was not enough to know what ethics was; they believed it important to know how to apply ethics, how to become more moral, how to shape the will — and not only the intellect — of morally aware and active human beings. They wanted to establish the relationship between true knowledge and the dilemmas and realities of the actual historical world in which they were participants.

And so in the Renaissance, out of the classical tradition and out of the classical texts of the liberal arts, the humanists created a basic educational system in the liberal arts. It was founded on classical texts; and it revolved around moral philosophy, the study of literature, of language, and of history. Such an education was conceived to be the basic and broad culture which would make people better citizens, better rulers, better people, better professionals.

It is of course paradoxical that what has come later to be seen by many as irrevelant, namely a training in the classics of the liberal arts, was for the humanists of the Renaissance the truly relevant — that their criticism of education in their own time should have been that it was too academic and that the bridge between learning on the one hand and the real world on the other was to be located in the classical liberal arts tradition. They saw the specializations of the university as irrelevant to the major preoccupations that people might have and to the major needs that people did have.

Now let us jump (quite unhistorically) to a recent era, namely the period of the 1960s, and examine once again a critique of education which became a critique of the contemporary world and a different vision of the future and of human purpose and capacity. We note that then the term *relevant* became the word against which to test the older understanding of the liberal arts. To simplify, one might say that those in the 1960s who attacked the undergraduate liberal arts curriculum and its institutions did so on the ground that they were *irrelevant*. These critics were maintaining that college faculties failed to make a connection between academic subjects and a real world that was full of social and political and moral difficulties. In a sense, they were maintaining that those ways of teaching liberal arts, or those kinds of liberal arts curricula, were not relevant to themselves either as moral beings or as citizens. So they saw themselves as actors in a world that required both a greater humaneness and a greater and more direct involvement in attending to the problems of that world. In a strange way, the conception of relevance and irrelevance came to be turned around, as it has been from time to time in the history of thinking about education, and the liberal arts tradition was attacked for its failure to relate academic learning to the problems of the real world.

Now this attack is different from another that has always existed: namely, the conviction that the liberal arts are not going to do much for you because they do not teach you to do anything. We always hear students or their families asking, "What do you do if you study history and decide you don't want to be a history teacher?" "What do you do after leaving campus if you study history of art or English literature?" How many of us are not familiar with that anxiety resulting from the belief that while college may be hoping to educate young people to be literate, imaginative, and perhaps even interesting, it may not equip them, as it were, to throw strikes?

There are, therefore, two different notions of relevance that have tended to surround controversy about the liberal arts. One is the notion of a higher relevance, the translation of the substance of an academic education into a more direct relationship with the shaping of individual minds and character and the capacity to relate those subjects to the larger concerns of contemporary life. The other represents a more specific connotation of relevance, concerned with how it is that the liberal arts may or may not help a student to a particular profession, or career, or vocation. These are familiar problems. In the debates today, there is a drawing away, I think, from the issues of the 1960s to issues that may more properly be called those of the 1980s. There is a turning back to the view that emphasizing the direct relevance of an undergraduate education to the specific dilemmas of social living or to the narrower preoccupation with a career must be harmful. There is, however, an increasing concern that within the contemporary circumstances of higher education in our society the greatest danger lies in narrow vocationalism rather than in an exaggerated regard for social relevance. So we find a revival of interest in thinking about the liberal arts. It is again attributed to making a diagnosis of what is wrong in our broader society; it begins with a critique of education.

The new diagnosis says education has become too fragmented, that in the chaos and confusion of the late 1960s curricula had lost their coherence and teachers their convictions, that any clarity of intellectual order and discipline as the central core of undergraduate education had faded away. Those failures, it is thought, had in part to do with the view that individuals should be free to choose how they would best be educated and that the academy should no longer prescribe an education — either because that was thought to be coercive or because the convictions which might guide such prescriptions had diminished or been lost entirely.

And so liberal education nowadays tends sometimes to become confused with the model of what is often called the "core" curriculum. The "core" curriculum may be an excellent approach to general or liberal education. Needless to say, we take great pride in that tradition and its maintenance at the University of Chicago. But we are, I think, in some peril of falling into the belief that it is a particular curriculum that characterizes a liberal education as opposed to a particular approach toward education. We should not confuse (and that is true for us who have "core" curricula as for those who do not) a syllabus or a curriculum with a liberal education *per se*. We must be careful not to reliteralize the conception of a liberal education as depending on one series of classical texts, or subjects, or requirements that may in the end provide one with a certificate. Coherence of purpose and of spirit are all-important in animating the liberal curriculum.

Nonetheless, it is, I think, extremely healthy that the new debate over "core" curricula and liberal arts education in our colleges should be again so active. It reflects something of a response to the threat that people see the liberal arts experiencing in a world where, it is feared, vocationalism and the pressure of economic circumstances may become overwhelming.

So much by way of background to an effort to talk a little bit about universities and liberal education. It is, of course, absurd to speak of higher education as a single entity. To do so would not only do violence to the realities of an educational system which has a variety of styles of education and of institutions within it, but it would also suggest that there *ought* to be a single form of higher education. We tend to talk that way; and at the same time, we assert the value of a pluralistic universe of education in which different styles of and approaches to education coexist.

We should not try to homogenize what ought rightly to be a very diverse universe. Nonetheless, when we speak of universities and their responsibilities for the liberal arts, we are taking in not only a broad range of higher education and a broad population of students, but we are talking about a tradition which, however differently it may be articulated, has some common presence in our universities that we need to be clearer about.

It is often difficult to remember that universities in our country are really so young. The university movement, properly speaking, is not much more than 100 years old. Historians of higher education tend to date the university movement either from the first Land Grant Act or from the opening of the Johns Hopkins University in 1876. It is often thought that if Johns Hopkins was the first true university that was designed as a research institution where undergraduate, graduate, and professional education came together, then the second might have been the University of Chicago, opened in 1892.

In that same period of time, many older institutions, ranging from the Yales and Harvards to others across the country, were growing from colleges into universities. Those colleges depended on the classical tradition. There took place also the enormous and fruitful growth of the university movement in the states, as in California, or Michigan, or Illinois. Some astonishing things were happening in the late nineteenth and early twentieth centuries. For example, at the University of Oregon, there was a teacher who held a combined professorship that included elocution, common law, physiology, and mechanical drawing. At South Dakota it is said that the professor of German, bookkeeping, penmanship, orthography, political economy, the United States Constitution, and the history of civilization also gave farm institute lectures in farm accounts, managed the men's dormitory, and was steward of an undergraduate boarding club. So, there were individuals who combined in themselves both the range of the arts and sciences and a good many vocational enterprises as well.

In the growth of the late nineteenth and early twentieth century, debates over the classical tradition, as opposed to graduate and professional training, became intense — as did debates over the classical tradition confronting an emerging scientific tradition. Ultimately in the twentieth century, the new developments of social science tended to encapsulate many of the older debates that had to do with the relationship between the liberal arts and other forms of "merely" academic or professional learning.

The second great period in the evolution of universities as we know them came after the Second World War. At that time, the view that universities in fact ought to do more, rather than less, came to prevail. The belief that growth in quality and growth in programs must go hand in hand stimulated competition among universities to become comprehensive. All that coincided with the explosion of a student population larger than it had ever been, including a significant group who, coming out of the war, were in many instances more mature, more motivated, more directed toward definite ends than earlier generations of students. This was a time, too, of extraordinary growth in the research capacity and facilities of our universities, and a time when the forms of graduate training and of major scholarship and research in American universities came to equal and surpass their counterparts elsewhere. Such growth was founded also on a faith — a faith in what education could achieve in the creation of better-educated people — and of a freer and better society that would encourage upward mobility and afford greater opportunities to all its people. It was founded also in the faith that in education lay the key to the future — that more and more educated people, that better and better education would inevitably produce an improved world.

The reaction in the sixties was not simply to the multiversity and to its perceived impersonality and lack of focus, but to what had come to be seen as a kind of bureaucratic institution that no longer spoke to what education was about and what education was for. Describing that time of growth, Malcolm Muggeridge said, "Higher education is booming in the United States; the gross national mind is growing along with the gross national product." That was, in a nutshell, the phenomenon that some of the students and faculty in the later sixties were protesting.

Many of us now in the academic world were trained and came to our professional maturity during an age of growth. We are now seeing the reversal of the assumptions that helped shape the institutions in which we live — a reversal of many of the expectations that seemed almost unquestionable in the age of growth. It is a long and painful process to review those expectations and assumptions and to attempt to reconcile the purposes in which we believe with new conditions that reflect the loss of opportunity and the modification of the faith that used to accompany not only education but the growth of education. This is a very inadequate description of the kind of internal spiritual crisis that confronts educators in universities at present, but perhaps it sets the context within which the new debates about liberal arts and vocationalism need to be considered.

In this situation, there resides a great danger of present-mindedness. In periods of constraint and difficulty, there is a tendency to think that the future will be exactly like the present. Therefore, one is tempted to narrow one's thinking about education and the appropriate development of educational institutions in two ways: first, to narrow down to the problems of survival in the present and not be able or feel able to look beyond; but secondly, and more seriously, one may diagnose the problems of the present and plan the future in such a way as to cure them, whereas the problems of the future as well as its opportunities may be quite different.

Let me give an instance of that. It seems to me that nowadays a number of institutions in the search for survival and in the search to become more "relevant" to their students' vocational needs, as they see those, are turning away from their own best beliefs about the nature of a liberal education at the undergraduate level. If that happens, they are not doing the service to those students that they ought — namely, to equip them to cope with complexity itself; to equip them to see the relatedness of things; to equip them to find ways of coming to judgments and of coming to understand the nature of choices that may lie before them, and others to whom they relate, in a way that makes sense, that has some logic, that has some coherence, and at the same time makes them responsible.

It is the responsibility of universities to keep alive subjects and ideas that may not be fashionable, that may not be popular. It is the responsibility of universities not only to protect and nurture these but, as it were, to create a higher relevance of the unfashionable and the unpopular. It is essential to sustain the studies of Egyptology and medieval history and sixteenth century French literature. That obviously does not mean all resources can be put into such areas or that there will not be enormous stringencies in the humanities. But if they are not to be preserved in universities, then that is a loss to civilization and a loss to the capacity and potential of generations to come, to education and scholarship in the future.

In the desire to deal as we need with problems that cry out for solutions and with constrictions that require adjustment, this fundamental sense of the nature of the university, which is also at the heart of the liberal arts tradition, needs a greater reassertion than ever before. Its educational objectives have to do with those ends that speak to the quality of intellectual competence, the ability to free oneself from the constraints of unexamined assumptions, the understanding of how to engage in the independent analysis and judgment of complexity in a remarkably complex world.

That may or may not suggest an instrumental understanding of liberal education. I believe it harmonious to think that the liberal arts are valuable in and of themselves and to believe that they also have consequences, intangible and not always realized but nonetheless real. I am led to yet another series of texts, which speak to what I think the liberal arts are in some sense ultimately about and to what our universities' obligations are to thinking about education, what it is about and what it is for, while acknowledging the very diverse ways in which given institutions may set about it.

One text comes from Robert Frost who said, "Education doesn't change life much; it just lifts trouble to a higher plane of regard." Another comes from Mark Twain who said that education consists "mainly in what we have unlearned." The third is from B. F. Skinner who said that "education is what survives when what is learned has been forgotten." Taken together, these three passages express the nature and the quality of what the liberal arts should mean to us today.

The character of the educational enterprise in the university requires a community of scholars and teachers who demand breadth in the approach to their subjects, self-conscious reflectiveness, a thoughtfulness about subjects under study, a respect for rigorous intellectual activity and its claims. Unless we reassert that conviction, our universities will become, whether we want it or not, vocational in the narrower sense and fail in their purpose and opportunity. Paradoxically, their influence and consequences in the real world will be far less — for with the dimming of the principles of learning, they will have lost the authority of their distinctive role.

Martin Trow is professor of sociology in the Graduate School of Public Policy of the University of California at Berkeley, where he directed the Center for the Study of Higher Education for more than a decade. After serving in the U.S. Navy during World War II, he graduated with a degree in mechanical engineering from Stevens Institute of Technology in 1947. After working briefly as an engineer, he did his graduate work at Columbia University, where he received his Ph.D. in sociology in 1957. He has taught at Columbia and at Bennington College, and has lectured at many universities in America and abroad. He has written extensively on education for American and European journals.

Professor Trow has been a fellow at the Center for Advanced Study in the Behavioral Sciences at Palo Alto, a visiting fellow at the Institute for Advanced Study at Princeton and a fellow at the Swedish Collegium for Advanced Study in the Social Sciences. He is a member of the National Academy of Education.

The ninth Henry Lecture was presented October 31, 1984, at the University of Illinois at Urbana-Champaign.

The University Presidency:
Comparative Reflections on Leadership

by Martin A. Trow
Director of the Center for Studies in Higher Education and
Professor of Sociology in the Graduate School of Public Policy
University of California, Berkeley

It is indeed an honor to be invited to give the Ninth David D. Henry Lecture here at the University of Illinois.* I have had the privilege of knowing David Henry, not only by reputation and through his writings, but also through a professional association. David Henry, in addition to his many other roles, was a member of the Carnegie Commission on Higher Education throughout its very active life. During those same years, I was a member of a small advisory committee that Clark Kerr brought together in Berkeley to review and comment on drafts of the many reports and recommendations that the commission issued during its lifetime.

Those reports and commission volumes are well known to all of us — in their blue and white covers stretching for several yards across our bookshelves. One of the commission's activities, indeed one of its most important, started as a recommendation in its report on the federal role in higher education, issued in 1968.[1] In that report, the commission, alone among major organizations in the world of higher education, came out strongly in favor of federal support in the form of aid to students rather than block grants to colleges and universities. During the next three years, there was intense activity on Capitol Hill, with the forces of the higher educational establishment, led by the American Council on Education, exerting all their efforts to have federal support come, if at all, directly to the institutions in the form of block grants linked to enrollments.

---
* Presented at the University of Illinois at Urbana-Champaign, October 1984.

In those years, these organizations and their leaders felt very strongly that higher education should present a united front on this issue and not break ranks. And David Henry, as a leader of organized higher education — past chairman of the ACE, past president of the National Association of State Universities and Land Grant Colleges, past president of the Association of Urban Universities, among others — was subjected to quite intense pressure, the precise nature of which only he knows, to break with the commission's position and join that of the higher education establishment. He did not — a decision that was both wise and courageous.

For as we know, the Higher Education Act of 1972 embodied David Henry's (and the Carnegie Commission's) position, and not that of the higher education establishment. It is very doubtful that the Congress at that time would have made any commitment to higher education beyond its support for research that took the form of institutional grants. If it had done so, it is quite certain that support, in that form, would not have survived the first year of the Reagan presidency. But in the form of student aid, federal support for higher education had, and has, a constituency and political support in Congress and throughout the country that saved the program, a program that in 1984 amounted to about $6.5 billion in grants and loans. Federal support for higher education through student aid is of enormous importance in extending access to American colleges and universities, public and private, large and small, to many who would not otherwise attend them. It was also the surest way of defending the autonomy of our institutions against the leverage that block grants would have given to the federal government when, in time, it surely would have wanted to exert its influence.

Many of David Henry's achievements are well known; this one is perhaps less well known, which is why I tell it here. It also illustrates the principle that leadership in higher education takes many forms, some of them occurring in private, in anonymity, and without due recognition.

University presidency

It is altogether fitting that in this lecture in honor of David Henry I speak of the university president and presidency. The subject has been touched on in several of the lectures in this series and was the chief subject of the seventh lecture in this series offered by Professor James March of Stanford University.[2] But perhaps the matter has not been quite exhausted. In this lecture I want to do the following:

First, I want to explore in somewhat general terms what we mean by "leadership" in universities, what its major dimensions may be.

Second, I will contrast the American university presidency with its counterpart in selected European countries.

Third, I will sketch the historical sources of the unique role of the university president that has developed in America.

Finally, I will try to identify some of the structures and institutional mechanisms through which the American university president does in fact take his initiatives, deploy his resources, exercise leadership.* One caveat: many of my remarks about the presidency of American universities also apply to four-year colleges, and particularly to the best of them. But this paper will focus on the role of the presidency as it can be seen in the great American research universities, perhaps thirty or so in all, of which the University of Illinois is a leading example. Moreover, when I refer to university *presidents,* I will be speaking mainly about chief campus officers — though both in the University of Illinois and in my own university, the chief campus officer is called *chancellor.* (The special problems of the heads of multicampus systems deserve a lecture, or a library, of their own.)[3]

Leadership in higher education, in large part, is the taking of effective action to shape the character and direction of a college or university, presumably for the better. That leadership shows itself chiefly along four dimensions: symbolic, political, managerial, and academic. Symbolic leadership is the ability to express, to project, indeed to seem to embody, the character of the institution — its central goals and values — in a powerful way. Internally, leadership of that kind serves to explain and justify the institution and its decisions to participants by linking its organization and processes to the larger purposes of teaching and learning in ways that strengthen their motivation and morale. Externally, a leader's ability to articulate the nature and purposes of the institution effectively helps to shape its image, affecting its capacity to gain support from its environment and to recruit able staff and students.[4] Political leadership refers to a leader's ability to resolve the conflicting demands and pressures of his many constituencies, internal and external, and in gaining their support for the institution's goals and purposes, as he defines them. Managerial leadership is the familiar capacity to direct and coordinate the various support activities of the institution. Ths includes good judgment in the selection of staff; the ability to develop and manage a budget, plan for the future, and build and maintain a plant. Academic leadership shows itself, among other ways, as the ability to recognize excellence in teaching, learning, and research; in knowing where and how to intervene to strengthen academic structures; in the choice of able academic ad-

---

* Here, as elsewhere, the male pronoun is used conventionally to refer to both male and female genders.

ministrators and in support for them in their efforts to recruit and advance talented teachers and scholars.

Any particular university president need not excel personally in all these dimensions of the presidency; leaders vary in how their talents and energies are distributed among these facets of academic life. Some are largely "external presidents," presenting the image of the institution to its external constituencies and seeking their support, while giving to a provost or dean the main responsibility for academic affairs and to a vice-president for administration the chief responsibility for internal management. Other presidents spend more of their time and attention on internal matters.

But however a leader fills the several dimensions of the role — in the definition of its character and purpose, in its quest for resources, in the management of its organization, or in the pursuit of ever higher levels of academic excellence — effective action in all areas requires that the president have the legal authority and resources to act, to choose among alternatives, even to create alternatives — in short, to exercise discretion. Without that discretion and the authority and resources behind it, a president or chancellor cannot exercise leadership, whatever his personal qualities.

So a discussion of leadership in American higher education must involve:

First, a comparison of the potential for leadership — the power and opportunities for discretionary decisions and action — of American college and university presidents as compared with their counterparts abroad.

Second, some suggestions as to why those differences exist — an historical reference which allows us to see more clearly how and why our institutions and their presidents are as they are.

And third, a somewhat closer examination of how American college and university presidents exercise power, and a look at some of the institutional characteristics and mechanisms that allow them to take initiatives.

Presidential influence

The American university presidency in recent years has had a bad press. Some of the most influential theorists about the organization and governance of higher education argue that colleges and universities are really ungovernable and that leadership in them is impossible. James March in his various writings, alone and with collaborators, has stressed the sheer chaos and unmanageability of organizations of higher education institutions characterized by "garbage-can decision processes," in which problems are more often evaded than solved. Colleges and universities, in his view, are prototypical "organized anarchies," characterized by ambiguous goals, unclear technology, and fluid participation.[5] Since their goals are ambiguous, nobody is sure where the organization is going or how it will get there. "Decisions are often by-products of activity that is unintended and unplanned...." They are not so much "made" as they "happen" — they are events in which problems, choices, and decision-makers happen to coalesce to form temporary solutions. From this point of view, "an organization is a collection of choices looking for problems, issues and feelings looking for decision situations in which they might be aired, solutions looking for issues to which they might be the answer, and decision-makers looking for work."[6] Such inept, leaderless organizations must be unable to initiate anything or innovate. As Cohen and March put it somewhat epigrammatically, "Anything that requires the coordinated effort of the organization to start is unlikely to be started. Anything that requires a coordinated effort of the organization in order to be stopped is unlikely to be stopped."[7] And if the university cannot be led or moved, then it follows in March and Cohen's view:

> "The presidency is an illusion. Important aspects of the role seem to disappear on close examination. In particular, decision making in the university seems to result extensively from a process that decouples problems and choices and makes the president's role more commonly sporadic and symbolic than significant."[8]

Similarly, George Keller cites Cohen, et al., approvingly in these words:

> "Universities love to explore processes and methodology but hate to make decisions.... Decisions in a university often get made randomly — by deans, legislators, a financial officer, the president."[9]

But oddly enough, all of Keller's illustrative cases show just the contrary, whether he is talking about planning for cuts at the University of California; or the survival of a private college in Maryland; or responses to cuts at the University of Minnesota, Carnegie-Mellon, or Teachers College, Columbia. These institutions are not exceptions. While each, of course, is unique — with its own configuration of problems and leaders — the capacity of American colleges and universities to adapt to new circumstances — whether demographic crisis, or budget cuts, or cultural and religious change, or technological explosions — is on the whole astonishing, and most of the gloomiest prophecies in recent decades have not been fulfilled. To take only one example: for at least a decade we have been told that, starting in 1979, enrollments in American colleges and universities would begin to decline — impelled inexorably by a decline in the size of the college age cohorts, a decline nationally of some 23 percent between 1979 and 1992 when these cohorts would be at their lowest levels. And according to these forecasts, the population of college age youth would not start to grow again until perhaps 1995. It is true that the number of high school graduates peaked in 1979 as predicted; by 1984, the size of the graduating class had already fallen some 13 percent below the 1979 peak. But to almost everyone's surprise, enrollments in colleges and universities nationally did not fall; on the contrary, they actually grew by 8 percent between 1974 and 1984 overall during this time of shrinking college age cohorts.[10]

Of course there are variations by region and by type of institution. But nevertheless, American colleges and universities have shown a remarkable capacity to respond both to recession and to declining age cohorts and have continued to attract growing numbers. I would suggest that much of this capacity to respond creatively and successfully to difficult — and in some cases, to life-threatening — circumstances must be attributed to the ability of institutional leaders to innovate, to motivate — above all, to lead. Our task is to learn more about the nature of the effective and creative leadership and how it works, rather than to assert, in the face of much contrary evidence, that it is impossible.

The thoughtful report of the Commission on Strengthening Presidential Leadership, *Presidents Make a Difference* (1984), is also rather gloomy about the state of the college and university presidency.[11] In the course of giving sound advice to institutions, presidents, and governing boards, the report identifies and discusses some recent and current developments which the commission believes have made the college and university presidency less attractive now to able people than it was formerly. Its authors are especially concerned with the growing constraints on the presidency — "more barbed wire around smaller corrals," as one of their informants put it. Oddly enough, though they reach the somber conclusion that "the American college and university presidency is in trouble," they note that "about one-fourth of all presidents [whom they interviewed] are quite satisfied with their situations (some are even euphoric); about one-half are clearly more satisfied than dissatisfied most of the time; and about one-fourth are dissatisfied — some even in despair."[12] But as one reads this report, one is struck by the fact that many of the problems that university presidents face, including some of those that have grown in difficulty recently, arise out of the very strength and centrality of the role — a role that has no real counterpart outside the United States.

Strong U.S. presidency compared with Europe

However constrained American college and university presidents may seem to American observers, however weak or ineffective they may appear to students of university organization, they look very strong by contrast with the power and influence of their "counterparts" abroad. The question may be raised of whether they *have* any true counterparts abroad. Certainly in any genuine sense they do not. The weakness of the "chief campus officer" — the rectors, vice-chancellors, or presidents — of European institutions of higher education arises out of the history and development of those universities. They arose, as we know, initially as guilds of masters — in some places, with important initiatives from students. European universities retained their character as corporate bodies of academics which in modern times came to be regulated, funded, and in varying degrees governed by agencies of the state. The basic power relationship in European higher education has been between the guild of academics and its chairman — the rector, on one side, and the relevant church authorities or governmental ministries on the other. Their discussions have centered on the issues of autonomy and support. The leading university academic officer — whether he is called rector, vice-chancellor, or president — was, and still is, largely a chairman of the corporate body, and on the continent and in the British ancient universities was elected, until recently, by the guild from among its own members. On the continent, he is still elected — though now from a wider and more politicized electorate.

There has been much talk in European academic circles since World War II about the desirability of strengthening the hand of the chief officer — making him more like his American counterparts, and indeed sometimes an effort to do that has been made merely by changing his name from "rector" to "president." But I do not think that European countries or institutions have actually gone very far in that direction, beyond the change of name. The broad reforms of higher education, introduced since 1968 in almost all European countries, have had the effect less of strengthening the president or rector than of weakening the professoriate — "democratizing" governance internally by giving more power and influence to the nonprofessorial staff and to students, and externally by increasing the influence of politicians, civil servants, and organized economic interest groups on institutional and regional governing boards. The literature on these reforms and reorganizations is not about more powerful institutional leadership, but about more and more complex internal group politics with central government trying to retain and extend its influence on the nature and direction of the institutions in the face of their claims to traditional autonomies and their newly expanded participatory democracy.

On the whole, informed Europeans admire the American university and recognize the role of its strong presidency in defending its integrity while responding to the many needs of the society which supports it. But their history and academic traditions make it impossible for them to duplicate our arrangements; indeed, in some countries, they seem to be moving in the opposite direction. For example, the current reform of French higher education has enormously complicated university government there; it has increased the number of central government councils which exercise direct control over aspects of university life, and it has increased the number of intermediate institutions standing between the university and central government. It has also further complicated and politicized the internal governance of each university.[13] The new Higher Education Guideline Law provides three elected committees to run the affairs of each university: a Board of Management, an Academic Council, and a Council in Charge of Studies and University Affairs. These councils vary in size from twenty to sixty people; members are elected every three years by a single electoral college composed of academic staff, technical personnel, students, and laymen through a system of proportional representation. The latter insures that external political parties and factions are firmly represented on these councils; indeed, it is a matter of principle that each group having an interest in the affairs of the university be represented in its councils, and those representatives are expected to function directly in the interests of the group which they represent. Moreover, these councils appear to have overlapping functions.

In addition, the law provides for five national councils to develop national policies and guidelines on every aspect of university life, as well as permitting new regional and department (county) organizations to coordinate policies at their levels. This is, I may say, a structure worthy of Rube Goldberg; it is difficult to imagine this machinery being able to reach any decisions about anything. I gather that thus far French universities survive largely by not implementing many of the new rules; but that is a precarious way to survive.

Matters are not quite so bad with respect to institutional leadership in the United Kingdom, often cited as the system nearest to the United States in its forms of university organization among European countries. But even there, the University Grants Committee (UGC), long a conduit of advice from the universities and of funds from central government, has more recently become a conduit of advice to the universities from central government along with reduced funds — advice which in recent years has hardened into directives regarding the organization and priorities of individual universities. Moreover, British vice-chancellors — the nearest equivalent to our own university president — have not on the whole been able to respond effectively to the political and economic challenges and stresses posed by the budget cuts of the 1980s.[14] Those cuts were distributed unevenly by the UGC among the several universities on criteria that have never been made clear nor justified. They were then distributed within each institution, usually in the academically least defensible way, in part across the board and in part by forced early retirement of senior staff — extremely expensive — and involving the loss of men and women who were often at the peak of their teaching and scholarly powers.

Historical perspective

So the comparative perspective on American higher education and its leadership is one of American exceptionalism, of a sharp contrast between the role of institutional leadership here as compared with that in almost every other modern society, as well as one of quite astonishing success. We can understand better the almost unique character of the American college and university presidency if we look at it in historical perspective. The strength of the university presidency in this country, as compared with its overseas counterparts, arose out of the weakness of the academic profession in America throughout most of our history in conjunction with the tradition of noninvolvement by federal government in education generally, and in higher education particularly.

These two factors — the weak academic guild and weak central government — are also related to the strength of lay boards as the chief governing bodies of colleges and universities. The lay board originated at Harvard, the first American university. The founders of Harvard, community leaders of whom most had studied at the University of Cambridge, had intended to carry on the English tradition of resident faculty control. The senior academic members of the Oxford and Cambridge colleges, the "dons," comprised then, as now, a corporate body which governed each of the constituent colleges that make up those ancient universities. But in the colonial United States, there simply were no scholars already in residence. Harvard had to be founded and not just developed. Without a body of scholars to be brought together who could govern themselves, the laymen who created the institution had to find someone to take responsibility for the operation of the infant university, and that person was the president. He was, in fact, the only professor to begin with, and he both governed and carried a major part of instruction himself, with some younger men to help. And this pattern lasted for quite a long time in each new institution — long enough to set governing patterns throughout our history. Harvard was established for more than eighty-five years, Yale for some fifty, before either had another professor to stand alongside its president. For a very long time, both before and after the American Revolution, many colleges and universities relied wholly on the college president and a few tutors who would serve for a few years and then go on to another career.[15]

To this set of historical facts we may attribute the singular role of the college and university president in American higher education. He combined in himself the academic role with the administration of the institution. The members of the lay governing boards from the very beginning have had other things to do and have delegated very large powers to the president whom they appointed — a president who did not until this century have to deal with a large or powerful body of academic peers. The American college and university president still holds his office wholly at the pleasure of the external board which appoints him. Most of the rest of the academic staff have tenure in their jobs. But the president of a college or university never has tenure, at least not as president (though he may return to a professorship if he has such an appointment in the institution). That lack of tenure in office partly accounts for the broad power the board delegates to him; they can always take it back, and often do.

So for a long time in American history there were very few who made academic life a career; as long as that was true, there was no real challenge to the authority of the president so long as he had the support of the lay board which governed the institution. This, of course, is quite unlike arrangements in most other countries. European universities, as we know, arose out of guilds — the corporations of doctors and masters and other learned men in Paris, Bologna, and elsewhere. And where they arose differently, as in the modern universities, the academics in their faculties claimed the same powers as their counterparts in the ancient universities. In America, by contrast, colleges and universities were created by a lay board and a president. This has had an enormous impact on the development of our institutions.

The near absolute authority of the American college president has been lost in most of our universities over time, especially with the rise of the research university and the emergence of a genuine academic profession in the last decades of the nineteenth century. In this century, and especially in the stronger universities, a great deal of autonomy over academic affairs has been delegated to the faculty and its senates. But the American college or university president remains far more powerful than his counterparts in European institutions, whose formal authority and power is shared with the professoriate, junior staff, government ministries, advisory boards, student organizations, and trade unions, and where the rector or vice-chancellor really is a political man — a power broker, a negotiator, a seeker for compromise without much power or authority of his own.

Faculty influence

The role of the faculty in the governance of the leading colleges and universitites in the United States is substantial and important, but it is as much a source of presidential power as a limitation on it. The two generations of presidential giants — White at Cornell, Eliot at Harvard, Angell at Michigan, Gilman at Hopkins, Harper at Chicago, Van Hise at Wisconsin, Jordan at Stanford, Wheeler at California, among others — the men who governed the great American universities between the Civil War and World War I, essentially created the American academic profession, a development which coincided with the emergence and growth of the great research universities. Those creative presidents flourished, however, before their universities had large numbers of specialized scholars and scientists with high prestige in American society as well as national and international reputations in their disciplines. Those presidents recruited distinguished scholars and scientists, paid them decent salaries, rewarded their scholarship and research, and thus created the faculty of the modern research university — a body of men and women who could meet them, collectively at least, as equals. The American academic profession and its instruments — the senates on campus and the AAUP and the various disciplinary associations nationally — were the institutionalized expression or reflection of those scholars and scientists brought together in the new research universities by this generation of great university presidents. It was the growth of that body of academics, increasingly aware of their collective importance to the university and to its supporters and constituents outside the university, that gave rise to the modern university faculty, determined to be treated as members and not merely as employees of the university. They thus came to be included in the governance of the universities, in a role which stressed their right to be consulted on matters of importance to them.

In the leading universities, both public and private — though matters are quite different in the second- and third-tier universities — what has evolved is a system of shared governance, marked by a degree of cooperation and mutual trust that has survived the political stresses of the 1960s; the demands for greater accountability from state governments of the 1970s; the growth of federal law and regulation; the consequent elaboration and formalization of procedures, recordkeeping, and reporting; and the explosion of litigation against the university over the past two decades. Despite all of these forces and the internal stresses they have engendered, academic senates and committees in the leading universities still gain the willing and largely unrewarded participation of active and leading scholars and scientists in the process of governance by consultation. The nature of this shared governance by consultation is extremely complicated and subtle, never adequately captured in the description of the formal arrangements which differ on every campus. Moreover, the power of the faculty varies sharply, depending on the status of the university and of its faculty.

It is sometimes suggested that a strong academic senate reduces the power of the president or chancellor. I believe, on the contrary, that a strong senate enhances the power of the president. An academic senate is, above all, an instrument for the defense of academic and scholarly standards in the face of all the other pressures and demands on the university and on its president. Senates function on the whole through committees; committees are, or can be, excellent bodies for articulating and applying academic values to a variety of conditions and issues that arise. They are splendid at saying "no"; they are poor instruments for taking initiatives or implementing them. By being consulted routinely on a wide variety of initiatives emanating from the office of the president, the senate may in fact give wise and useful advice. But above all, it makes itself, and faculty sentiments, felt by giving or withholding its approval and legitimacy to presidential initiatives. Without that consultation and support, the relation of president and faculty would be largely adversarial — which is what we often see where the senate has been replaced by a faculty union, or where the faculty and president are deeply at odds. And there the power of the president is certainly diminished.

Of course, there are frictions between senate and president; the relationship at its best is marked, in Jacques Barzun's words, by "the good steady friction that shows the wheels are gripping." In such a happy relationship, faculty members recognize that just as the effectiveness of the president depends in large part on a strong senate, so also does the strength of the senate depend on a strong president. It is *not* a zero sum game. For much of the senate's power is exercised through its advice to and influence on the president: where *he* has little power, *they* have little power. Effective power then lies outside the institution altogether, in the hands of politicians or ministries, as in European nations or some American states.

Resources for leadership

I have suggested on historical and comparative grounds that the president of a leading American college or university can exercise leadership: symbolic, political, intellectual, and administrative. But what are his resources for the exercise of leadership, especially when looked at in comparative perspective? What I will say here is familiar to all and yet it is often dismissed or discounted by commentators except when they are actually describing specific leaders and policies.

First, a president has substantial control over the budget of his institution and its allocation. Of course the president's discretion is constrained by the very large fraction of the budget committed to tenured faculty salaries and to support services that must be funded if the institution is to continue to function. But looked at comparatively, the president of a leading American university has relatively large power over his budget and its allocation. In a public university, he usually works with a block grant; thus, he can view the budget as a whole and make internal adjustments subject to the constraints that I have mentioned. By contrast, most European institutions are funded by central state authorities on what is closer to a line-item budget — sums are earmarked for particular chairs and the support staff around them and to particular services, such as a library. The rector or president ordinarily has little power over these internal allocations of funds. Moreover, in the United States it is now widespread practice, if not quite universal, that faculty vacancies resulting from death or retirement revert to the president's office and are not the property of the departments where the vacancy occurred. This reversion of resources permits the president and his associates over time to modify the internal distribution of faculty places in response to changing student demand or market demand, to developments in the disciplines themselves, or to his own ideas about the right mix of fields and subjects.

Academic autonomy is related, if not perfectly, to the multiplicity of funding sources.[16] Here again, by contrast with their European counterparts, American universities are funded in a variety of ways, which in itself gives a president a certain power to bargain from strength in the face of demands from one or another of his funding sources. Even such public universities as the University of California are not state supported so much as "state-aided." The University of California gets about two-fifths of its current operating budget from state sources; about 15 percent from federal grants and contracts; about 13 percent from fees, tuition, gifts and endowment; and one-third from various enterprises such as teaching hospitals, educational extension, and sales of educational services.[17]

But in addition to the sheer multiplicity of sources, some of them are more discretionary than others. The use of unearmarked private contributions, research overhead funds, some of the return on the endowment, is largely at the discretion of the president or chancellor, though over time, of course, those discretionary funds become encumbered by expectations if not by formal programmatic commitments. Programs and people supported by such discretionary funds come to expect that they will continue to be supported. But presidents and their staffs can vary the levels of those commitments, especially if they do so incrementally, and thus maintain a genuine degree of discretionary power over their allocations.

Even where discretion is not total, it may be large within a category. For example, a large sum comes to Berkeley and to our sister campuses through what are called "student registration fees," which are remarkably like what is called "tuition" elsewhere except that they are supposed to be spent on some kind of direct service to students, and not for the support of instruction or research. But "student services" is a very broad rubric indeed, and gives a chancellor at Berkeley equally broad discretion for shaping the mix of such services as between a learning center, medical services, counseling services, intramural athletics, recruitment and admissions, and various forms of remedial education and outreach to the secondary school system, among others.

The very size of student support services in American universities, as compared with those overseas, increases the power of presidents; where academic staff is largely tenured and their programs and departments difficult to modify except slowly and incrementally, the president has far greater (though never total) freedom to restructure support services whose staff members are not tenured (though increasingly unionized). These large support staffs report to someone directly in the president's office, and they constitute a substantial body of resources and people whom the president can draw on in support of his own priorities — again within certain political, legal, and normative constraints. A large staff provides the resources to put behind the president's own ideas about a stronger development office, or larger affirmative action programs, or whatever it is he may think important.

But the discretionary resources built into student services are only part of the staff resources available to American university presidents. In the United States, the great authority of lay governing boards — much of it delegated to the president, together with the relatively smaller role of central government — ensured that as the public universities grew and needed larger administrative staffs, those staffs would be extensions of the president's office rather than civil servants responsible to a faculty body or to state authorities. As a result, the strong president, supported by his own large administrative staff, has been able to preserve much autonomy and power inside the university. Having his own internal staff allows the college or university president to deal with state authorities with equal skill and expertise, rather than as a scholarly amateur against a body of professional planners and managers. Several points about this large internal staff follow:

Many, and most of the top, staff people owe their appointments to the president they serve and hold those appointments at his discretion. In some institutions there are "untouchables" on the staff, who have independent ties to the board or powerful alumni; these sometimes constitute a problem for new presidents. But on the whole, few members of the administrative staff have any formal or informal security of employment, and even they owe their advancement, and sometimes their jobs in periods of contraction, to the sitting president. They are for the most part his employees, in a part of the university that much more closely resembles the hierarchical structures of bureaucracies than the collegial structures of departments and research centers. Presidential leadership is often found in programs that rest largely on this administrative staff rather than on the reshaping of the academic programs directly; and that, I think, is because that is where so much of his discretionary resources lie.

These support staffs under the president's direction and leadership can also develop programs which further increase his discretion. For example, strengthening a development office, increasing the effectiveness of market research and student recruitment, writing better proposals for government or foundation grants all increase the discretion of top administrators. These activities and funds can provide the staff support for new academic programs, new links to secondary schools, remedial courses, creative connections with local industry and other colleges and universities. They give the president the needed resources to create priorities, to be an entrepreneur, and to take advantage of opportunities as they arise.

In the United States, the president of a college or university is the link between "the administration" and its support services, on the one hand, and the faculty and its programs of teaching, learning, and research, on the other. And here again the American college and university differs fundamentally from its overseas counterparts. Almost everywhere else, alongside the rector or president stands a registrar, a "curator," an administrative officer who is not appointed by the president and who is not really responsible to him but is appointed by the lay governing council or by a government ministry. In the U.K., a vice-chancellor plays a large role in the appointment of the registrar, but the appointment is rather like a senior civil service post and ordinarily continues beyond the term of any sitting vice-chancellor. And that sharp separation of the academic (and symbolic) leadership from the day-to-day management and administration of the institution enormously reduces the authority and discretion of the chief campus officer of European universities, as compared with his American counterparts.

In addition to the support staff I have spoken of, the American college or university president also appoints the chief academic officers: the vice-president for academic affairs, the provost, the deans and through them, the department chairmen, who are both heads of their departments and administrative officers. The president appoints them, and he can replace them. Of course he cannot do that frivolously or too often without loss of respect and credibility. Nevertheless, the fact that the president appoints the senior academic administrators, unlike his counterparts overseas (and the British case is intermediate in this regard), gives him a degree of leverage over changes in the academic program: for example, the opportunity to influence the balance of subjects, the subdisciplines represented, and, above all, the quality and character of new appointments.

Another consequence of the fact that the president appoints his senior administrative colleagues — his cabinet, so to speak — is that he largely defines their areas of authority and responsibility; they are not inherent in the job, or office, or in fixed regulations of the institution or ministry. University presidents in the United States (unlike their European counterparts) can and indeed often do change the administrative structures under them in the service of their own purposes and conceptions of the interests of the institution. And that restructuring — ordinarily at the beginning or early in the tenure of a president — may be one of his most creative acts. At Berkeley, for example, the current chancellor brought many student support services under the authority of a Vice-Chancellor for Undergraduate Affairs, an *academic* officer, thus breaking down the previous insulation between student services and the academic program. Moreover, presidents can modify the charge and scope of responsibility of any given academic administrator in response to the interests, talents, and capacities of the individual whom he appoints to a post, as well as to new problems and opportunities that develop around it. In addition, leaders can create decision making structures *ad hoc,* in response to different issues that arise.

If we ask what is the decision-making process at a college or university, we have to answer: "It depends on the issue." Different people and interests are brought together to solve or address different problems. But *who* is brought together to address *what* problems is determined chiefly by the president, and that indeed is an important area for the exercise of his discretion and the demonstration of his capacity for leadership. Should a senior academic officer be brought into a discussion of changes in admission procedures, which often conceal changes in academic standards? Should faculty members or academic senate committees be involved in decisions about the athletic program? Should a university financial officer be involved in discussions about a change in the requirements for graduation? What interests, what expertise, what individuals and perspectives should be brought together to deal with a particular problem; at what point will a greater diversity of perspectives not improve and inform a decision, but paralyze it? Those are among the most consequential judgments and decisions that a college or university president makes.

There is another mechanism of presidential power and initiative — one that lies directly at the heart of the academic enterprise, but which I think has not been adequately studied or discussed by students of American college and university life — and that is the power of a president to take a department or program "into receivership." Various observers have emphasized that colleges and universities are organizationally "bottom-heavy," in that expertise, both with respect to teaching and research, is located among the faculty members and in the departments. This is certainly true, and under ordinary conditions, college and university presidents are wise not to interfere in the private life of departments: in what and how they teach, what they study, whom they appoint, and whom they promote. The autonomy of departments, rooted in their expertise, is an important constraint on the power of administrators, including presidents.

But in American colleges and universities that autonomy can be overridden and set aside when something goes wrong: when, for example, factional fights within a department make it ungovernable, or prevent new appointments from being made, or block all promotions; or other tendencies and events lead to a decline in the unit's standing in the periodic national ranking of departments, or a fall-off in its external research support, or a degree of politicization that affects the quality of instruction, or a loss in the department's ability to attract able students or junior staff. These are among the reasons that lead presidents to take departments into receivership. When they do, they take the government and management of the unit out of the hands of the department members themselves, and of their chairman, and put it in the hands of others, with a clear understanding on how to proceed and what to do. The caretaker may be a person from another related department, or from the same discipline in another university, or even a committee of leading scientists and scholars from within the same institution. In my own university, this has happened to five or six departments over the past decade, including most recently to all of the biological sciences in some twenty-five departments and schools.[18] And like all drastic sanctions, the power to put departments into receivership is a powerful threat as well as an act and affects behavior even when it is not employed.

Control over the budget and especially over the discretionary resources in "student services"; the relatively large staff appointed by and responsible to the president; his power to set the institution's priorities, define problems, and specify who is to solve them; his power to take departments into receivership are some of the organizational resources and mechanisms for intervention and change by which leadership can be exercised in American research universities.

Speculation on the presidency

To sum up, I think it would be useful to get beyond the descriptions of universities as "organized anarchies" engaged in "garbage-can processes of decisionmaking." I doubt that these descriptive categories have any real influence over what college and university presidents actually do, but they stand in the way of a clearer description and understanding of the elements and functions of leadership in higher education.

Let me close with a query: If indeed the presidency of great research universities is as strong and effective as I claim, why has it had such a bad press in recent years? Why is it seen as weak, as ineffective, and as unattractive as it is portrayed? Some speculations, if not explanations, may be helpful here.

First, much of the gloomiest writing about university leadership addresses the situation of weaker second- and third-rank institutions. In the American system — marked by a very high level of competitiveness among institutions for students, for faculty, for resources, for prestige and rank, the power of the leading universities as models, both as organizations and as normative communities, is very great. All universities judge themselves by the standards and criteria of the leading universities and share their high expectations regarding research, graduate work, and institutional autonomy. But those second- and third-ranking institutions do not command the resources of the leading ones: their financial support, both public and private, their libraries and laboratories, their eminent faculties — all the traditions of autonomy that the leading institutions have gained over the years. It may be that the difficulties of university presidents in most institutions commonly arise out of the tension between their high aspirations and inadequate resources, and their resulting sense of relative failure when they compare themselves to Harvard, to Stanford, to Berkeley, or Michigan, or Illinois.

In addition to the costs of this kind of "relative deprivation" are the often frustrating experiences of university presidents, even in the leading institutions. The corral does sometimes seem smaller, the barbed wire higher than it was, or at least as it is remembered.[19] It may be that the presidency of a research university is a more effective, than attractive, position. In one of the most poignant commentaries on the role, the report of the Commission on Presidential Leadership quotes one president as follows:

> On any issue I will enjoy an incredibly high ninety to ninety-five percent of faculty support. Even so, five percent are dissatisfied with my decision, and they remember. On the next issue, I'll again enjoy the same ninety to ninety-five percent support, but the five to ten percent of dissenters will be a different group, and they, too, will

remember. Eventually one manages to make at least one decision against the convictions of virtually every member of the faculty. By recognizing and providing an outlet for such accumulated discontent, the formal evaluation process merely increases the speed by which courageous decision makers are turned over. This does nothing for attracting the best people into the jobs.[20]

This "accumulation of discontent" threatens to make the aggregate of many small successes into one big failure. And the inexorable erosion of support that this process describes casts its pall over both the role and the office.

Moreover, university presidents are more likely to underplay their power and effectiveness and exaggerate the importance of the process of "shared governance" of which they are a part than they are to claim undue credit for their achievements. In this democratic — indeed populist — age, the towering figures of the heroic age of the university presidency would surely find themselves under attack as authoritarian, power-driven, and without a sensitive concern for the interests of their varied constituencies in the university.

One example only: Clark Kerr, who gave the first David Henry lecture in this distinguished series, was, as we all know, a very strong chancellor of the University of California, Berkeley, from 1952 to 1958 and an equally strong president of the University of California system from 1958 to 1967. In both those roles, he had an enormous impact on the institutions that he led — for example, he shaped the quite distinct characteristics of the new campuses of the university which were established during his tenure as president. And yet, in his seminal book, *The Uses of the University*, perhaps the most illuminating essay on the modern research university, Kerr, after some nostalgic references to the giants of the past, observes that in his own time a university president is likely to be "the Captain of the Bureaucracy who is sometimes a galley slave on his own ship."[21] And he quotes Allan Nevins' observations that the type of president required by the new university — the "multiversity," as Kerr called it — "will be a coordinator rather than a creative leader . . . an expert executive, a tactful moderator. . . ." In Kerr's own words, "he is mostly a mediator."[22]

This, I suggest, is at odds with the realities of university leadership — both as Clark Kerr employed it and as it now exists. Of course, leadership may be more visible and dramatic during periods of growth and expansion, and not all presidents carry to the role the talents that Kerr did. And of course, coordination and mediation were important parts of the job, then as now. But boldness, the undertaking of initiatives, the acting by a president on and through the institution in the service of his own conception of its nature and future — in my view, all of that does not have the weight and emphasis in Kerr's analysis of university leadership that it did in his own exercise of leadership. Kerr's analysis reflects his concern (reflected again in the report of the Commission on Strengthening Presidential Leadership that he chaired) regarding the decline of institutional leadership as a result of the growth of countervailing forces and complex power centers within and around the university. I believe his analysis also reflects his sense that modern university leaders, if they are to be effective, must keep a low profile, must appear to be finding a "sense of the meeting" rather than imposing themselves on the institution and taking important initiatives within it. If we compare the modern university president to those of the heroic age, we find today more problems, more restraints, even more resources — more of everything, except authority. The exercise of authority is today often attacked as "authoritarian," and successful presidents have learned the trick of exercising authority without appearing to do so — to lead while appearing to follow, or facilitate, or mediate, or coordinate.

Of course the interplay among the characteristics of the person who occupies the office, the role, and the university's institutional environment is tremendously complex, and successful leadership today requires high skills and careful attention to the process of governance. And finally, even when the presidency is successful, troubles multiply and opposition accumulates; it is perhaps, inevitably, a case of "doing better and feeling worse."

This may be why presidents tend to underplay their own effectiveness. But why do observers and analysts do likewise? I have already set forth some of the reasons, but there is one other, and that is the apparent anarchy of intertwined purposeful policies in universities. I suspect that observers have been looking at the university president's role as if it were a cross-section of a thick cable, made up of many differently colored strands or wires, each strand representing another program or activity, and all together in cross-section representing a heterogeneous collection of issues, solutions, and problems, showing little coherence or purpose. But in the research university, this model is misleading. For if this rope is cut along the dimension of time, we see that each strand extends backwards and forwards, moving along in its own coherent, purposeful, even rational way — each marked by its own set of purposes which are largely insulated from other strands, even as they intertwine.[23] So what appears as a random or haphazard collection of events, problems, evasions, and solutions, when viewed in cross-section at a given moment, looks more like a set of purposeful programs — each being pursued in relative isolation within the boundaries of the same institution, when viewed along the dimension of time. And the variety of these programs in their purposes and participants will be greater the more comprehensive and varied the role of the university in society-at-large.

It is this multiplicity of activities, governed by different norms and purposes and pursued in different ways, that defines the comprehensive university. And it is of some interest to consider how these activities, apparently governed by different and even incompatible values, can be pursued on the same campus, under the general authority of the same president. The key lies in the institutional insulations of activities governed by different values, and the ways in which these activities are brought together in the office of the president. One common situation finds presidents serving what appear to be the mutually incompatible values of academic excellence and social equity — the latter taking the form of increased access to the institution of underrepresented groups. In Berkeley currently, the commitment to excellence is represented by a major reform of the biological sciences very much keyed to strengthening modern currents in biology, both in research and teaching. This involved a major intervention by the chancellor with the advice and support of leading biologists on campus, an intervention that required the creation of new institutional forms and the temporary but substantial reduction of the power and autonomy of the existing biological departments to control their own faculty recruitment, graduate training, and the like. At the same time, other units of the chancellor's office were engaged in major efforts to upgrade the secondary education of minority groups in the cities surrounding Berkeley from which many of its undergraduates are drawn. These activities come together in the office of the chancellor, and only there — although they are carried on quite separately and in many ways are highly insulated from one another. It is doubtful if any of the distinguished biologists involved in the renewal of their discipline at Berkeley knows very much about the outreach programs into the Oakland secondary schools, or the outreach staff know anything about developments in the biological sciences on campus. In the particular circumstances of Berkeley at the moment — and I suspect this is true much more widely, it is necessary for the university to be serving the values both of excellence and of equity and to be seen to be doing so. How that is done depends very much on the sensitivity of a university leader both to his external political environment and to the internal groups and values with whom he must work, most notably the faculty.

There is, of course, an apparent contradiction in the values that govern these two kinds of programs. But these two strands of policy, differently colored and serving different ends and values, are not competitive but supportive — closely intertwined as they move along the dimension of time. It is, I suggest, the task of university leadership to tend both to these strands of university policy and to weave them together. And if that is done effectively, it may not be visible to observers of the office of the president or chancellor — observers who may be more impressed by the illogic or inconsistency of the values served than by the skills and initiative that enter into their accommodation within the same institution. Of course, incoherence and the loss of institutional integrity always threaten the American research university which says "yes" to almost all claims on its energies, resources, and attention. But it is precisely the nature of leadership in American universities and the broad conceptions of its power and the resources at its disposal that enable the university president or chancellor to give coherence, character, and direction to an institution so large in size and aspiration, so various in its functions and constituencies, so deeply implicated in the life of learning and of action, with links to so many parts of the surrounding society. These great research universities are among the most successful institutions in the world. They could not be if their presidents could not give them direction, as well as the capacity for responding to what is almost always an unanticipated future. It is in the office of the president that the necessary resources and opportunities lie.

Problems of the presidency

Problems with which we have resources to cope may also be seen as opportunities. The great research universities currently face a series of such problems (or opportunities) which are uniquely the responsibility of their presidents, however useful their aides and staff may be. Each of us will have his or her own short list of grave problems that face university presidents, and these lists will change over time. But my own list would include at least these, though not necessarily in this order of importance:

1. There is the problem each president faces of accommodating to or reconciling demands for broadened access by students from historically underrepresented groups with the maintenance of the highest standards in teaching and research. This is the familiar tension in education between equity and excellence, both served in different ways within the same institution, and to differing degrees by different institutions.

2. There is the problem of the evolving relations between research universities and industry. The question presents itself as how to serve industry while using its funds, research facilities, and know-how for the university's own purposes, at the same time maintaining the unique qualities — the very integrity — of the university as a place committed to the pursuit of truth in an atmosphere of open inquiry and free communication.

3. There are the problems created for the university by the very rapid growth of scientific knowledge, and the impact of that growth on the organization of the schools and departments of science and technology, and on the physical facilities in which science is done within the university.

4. Closely linked to the third is the problem of maintaining a flow of new scientists and scholars into departments and research labs, without institutional growth, and with a largely tenured and aging faculty which is not retiring in large numbers until the 1990s or later.

5. On the other side of the campus, there is the problem of sustaining the humanities and the performing arts — that is, of maintaining the crucial balance of subjects within the university — in face of the expansion of scientific and technological knowledge and the growing attractiveness of professional training, especially at the undergraduate level.

6. And finally, the problem on which perhaps all others depend: The defense of freedom of speech and of academic freedom on campus in the face of intense pressure from vocal minorities of students and faculty who, unlike the rest of us, do not have to pursue the truth since they already possess it and who are loathe to permit others with whom they disagree to express and propagate what they view to be error and pernicious doctrines. (The theological language here is intentional.)

What a list! Yet we expect presidents to cope with large problems, as no other national university system does, because in fact our society gives them the authority and the resources to cope. There are never enough resources, in their view, yet by and large, they do cope. It is still in part a mystery how they cope so successfully, when so much of the theory of organizational leadership tells us they cannot and should not.

But I think that the office of the university president has not been properly appreciated; it has been the object more of compassion and criticism than of understanding. The university presidency deserves understanding, though I suspect that incumbents will continue to speak of it deprecatingly and, with good reason, as fraught with difficulties and constraints. And meanwhile, under their leadership in that extraordinary office, our research universities go on from strength to strength.

References

1. Carnegie Commission on Higher Education, *Quality and Equality: New Levels of Federal Responsibility for Higher Education,* New York: McGraw-Hill, December 1968.
2. James March, "How We Talk and How We Act: Administrative Theory and Administrative Life," Seventh David D. Henry Lecture, Urbana-Champaign, Illinois: The University of Illinois at Urbana-Champaign, 1980.
3. On multi-campus systems, see Eugene Lee and Frank Bowen, *The Multi-campus University: A Study of Academic Governance,* New York: McGraw-Hill, 1971.
4. On the distinction between organizations and institutions and the role of leadership in the defining purpose and mission, see Philip Selznick, *Leadership in Administration,* Evanston, Illinois: Row, Peterson, 1957, esp. pp. 5-28.
5. M. Cohen and J. G. March, *Leadership and Ambiguity,* New York: McGraw-Hill, 1974, p. 3.
6. Ibid., p. 81.
7. Ibid., p. 206.
8. Ibid., p. 2
9. George Keller, *Academic Strategy,* Baltimore: Johns Hopkins, 1983, p. 86.
10. For these figures and projections, see *Higher Education and National Affairs,* February 24, 1984, and *Chronicle of Higher Education,* April 4, 1984.
11. The Commission on Strengthening Presidential Leadership, *Presidents Make a Difference,* Washington, D.C.: The Association of Governing Boards, 1984.
12. Ibid., pp. xix and xviii.
13. See Guy Neave, "Strategic Planning, Reform and Governance in French Higher Education," *Studies in Higher Education,* Vol. 10, No. 1, 1985; and Alain Bienayme, "The New Reforms in French Higher Education," *European Journal of Education,* Vol. 19, No. 2, 1984.

14. See for example, Maurice Kogan, "Implementing Expenditure Cuts in British Higher Education," in Rune Premfors (ed.), *Higher Education Organization,* Stockholm: Almqvist and Wiksell, 1984.
15. See Frederick Rudolph, *The American College and University,* New York: Alfred A. Knopf, 1962, pp. 161-166.
16. See Martin Trow, "Defining the Issues in University-Government Relations," *Studies in Higher Education,* Vol. 8, No. 2, 1983.
17. Private communication, University of California Budget Office.
18. See Martin Trow, "Leadership and Organization: The Case of Biology at Berkeley," in Rune Premfors (ed.), *Higher Education Organization,* Stockholm: Almqvist and Wiksell, 1984.
19. The phrase is drawn from the Commission on Strengthening Presidential Leadership, op. cit.
20. Ibid., p. 54.
21. Clark Kerr, *The Uses of the University,* Cambridge, Massachusetts: Harvard University Press, 1963, p. 33.
22. Ibid., p. 36.
23. This image, and the next few paragraphs, are drawn from my essay "Leadership and Organization: The Case of Biology at Berkeley," op. cit., pp. 166-167.

Responses, Questions, and Discussion

Thomas E. Everhart, Chancellor at Urbana-Champaign: Thank you very much, Martin. As a new chancellor, I must say I am tremendously encouraged. You know, after a few months, you begin to wonder if you can do anything useful, and you said that if I'm wise, perhaps I can. We will now turn to our panelists, president of the University of Illinois, Stan Ikenberry; Professor Joe Burnett, Dean of our College of Education; and Professor David Whetten from Commerce and Business Administration. They will comment, briefly, on Martin Trow's remarks and give you their own perspectives. We will proceed in the order given in the program; thus, we'll start with President Ikenberry.

Response by Stanley O. Ikenberry

President, University of Illinois

Professor Trow, that was a splendid statement. It's one of the most insightful analyses of the university presidency I have heard. There are two or three areas in which I am in special agreement and would like to emphasize.

First, I think the typologies of leadership you used throughout the paper are helpful. We always hear the need to distinguish between leadership and management. Your typologies are helpful in further underlining that distinction, particularly your use of the concept of symbolic leadership. I'm not sure "symbolic" is the term I would have chosen, but I think you are driving at a concept too frequently ignored in the academic enterprise. That is the responsibility of the president, the chancellor, and many other academic leaders within the institution, both administrative and faculty leaders, to help the university articulate the value system for which it stands. The University is a place of the mind and the spirit — values. Therefore, one of the key aspects of leadership, and one that falls more heavily on the president and the chancellor than on any other leader in the institution, is to help the university to articulate to its broader publics what it believes and what it stands for. The symbolic, managerial, and academic components of leadership, I believe, are helpful in understanding this issue.

I, too, believe that several analyses of the health of the American university presidency are much too pessimistic. The reports of our demise are premature. The "garbage-can theory" suffers from this pessimistic view, as you pointed out so well. It seems to fail to grasp the complexity of the process. Tom Everhart was helpful in making the analogy that many scientific and other phenomena appear irrational or random, but after study we find purpose and order; we don't see irrationality, but functioning in terms of some fairly well understood principles or theory. The "garbage-can theory" fails to comprehend the rationality, fragmentary as it may be, that underlies the process.

The recent Kerr commission report also was a bit more pessimistic than I would have expected. Turn for a moment to the question of power. There are two very valid ways of looking at the power of the presidency. One is to say, the power of the president is rather limited; particularly it is limited from the perspective of the president when confronted with the expectations of the academic community and the power those outside the academic community tend to impute to the presidency. The president, at least this president, many times feels impotent to respond to the expectations that others would bring to the office, and he says to the trustees, or to the faculty, or to the governor, or to the legislature, "Very frankly, that's not within my power"; and many times, it is not.

I am convinced that we tend frequently to go outside of the university to find a president or chancellor precisely because it is easier to impute mythical qualities of power and wisdom to someone we know little about than to someone we know as a mere human being.

On the other hand, there are fundamental powers of the presidency, and these include the ability to set the agenda, to help create options, and to provide flexibility. When we talk about the weakened university presidency, we're referring more particularly to the failure on the part of the presidents to exercise the initiatives they do have, particularly as it relates to shaping the agenda of the university, whether it be in terms of symbolic, managerial, or academic issues. I'm not sure that I would agree that this is more prevalent in the smaller, academically weaker institutions than it is in the major universities, although I suspect on balance larger, stronger universities are more capable of attracting and retaining the strong leadership that may be needed. The results of presidential failure to shape the agenda and other leadership vulnerabilities fall equally on large, complex research universities, as well as the smaller ones.

Your point on the difference between the effectiveness of the university presidency and the degree of job satisfaction of the incumbents is an important point. It's not necessary for a university president to be happy and effective at the same time. Sometimes it isn't a very satisfying, happy, pleasant job, but the president can, at the same time, still be effective. The ability to make the distinction between satisfaction and effectiveness, particularly in analyses of the university presidency, is an important distinction. There is a tendency to confuse a low level of job satisfaction of presidents with presumed ineffectiveness.

Let me conclude by saying that the capacity of presidents and chancellors and other leaders in universities to see problems as opportunities is one of the special gifts of leadership. The values for which a president stands, the values for which an institution such as a university stands, are many times defined most vividly as a result of the battles and the struggles a president chooses to pursue. There are times where a president chooses to take off his coat, throw it in the road, and say, "This far, no further." It is sometimes through the act of confrontation that a president and a university begin to adapt and change and define values in precise terms. The same can be true when the president tackles managerial problems and exercises academic leadership. The president may have a severe problem in a particular academic college or department and, for its good and the good of the university, may need to say, "This department is bankrupt at the moment; or it is in receivership; or, in short, the conventional rules no longer apply and something must be done."

Opportunities to exercise presidential leadership come through problem-solving. These are the actions of real leaders and effective presidents.

I enjoyed your paper and appreciate this chance to respond.

Response by Joe R. Burnett

Dean, College of Education
University of Illinois at Urbana-Champaign

Let me say at the outset of my remarks that, especially as a dean, I have never had any reason to doubt the existence of considerable power for leadership in the university presidency, in the university chancellorship, or in the various university vice-chancellorships! Probably it takes the relative powerlessness of a deanship to see the great power of these offices, something perhaps not possible from the purely professorial role championed by people such as Cohen and March.[1]

As with our speaker, I also wonder about perspectives which say, in effect, that things would go relatively unchanged no matter which actors were placed in the top administrative roles of universities. For this reason I was pleased to hear Professor Trow speculate about how these perspectives might have received such wide coinage. As I understand his account, there are essentially three reasons:

1. There genuinely is not much potential for leadership at some institutions — those second- and third-tier ones suffering "relative deprivation" of resources;

2. There is an "apparent anarchy" in even the first-rate institutions which can mislead those not familiar with the complexity of the mega- or multiversity;

3. There is a tendency of presidents to underplay their power and influence as a means of keeping the low profile useful for being effective.

I would like to suggest an additional reason, one which might be closely associated with the third one just mentioned. It is the existence of an aspect of the professorial mentality which is always on guard against academic administration. Thus, Beneget, et al., interpret Cohen and March as reflecting "a certain archiness" (as an arch-villain) — the effect of which, perhaps, is "to help arm the professoriate against a president's zealousness...."[2] Such an archiness would be in a grand academic tradition, no grander representative of which can be found than Thornstein Veblen. Veblen's *The Higher Learning in America*[3] — which Veblen once thought of calling "A Study in Total Depravity"[4] — dealt with college/university presidents as, at best, irrelevant to the proper functioning of research and scholarship. More generally he viewed them as harmful to creative research. He spoke of them as "Captains of Erudition," as being as damaging to academe proper as their industrial and business analogues, the "Captains of Solvency," were to the inventive spirit, the Spirit of Workmanship, in the laboratory and workplace.

David Riesman, himself a student of the university presidency, writes that Veblen's belief "that a university bureaucracy is not necessary still hangs on...."[5] One could venture that, to the extent a university president wanted to keep a low profile, this aspect of the professorial mentality might serve him or her well. But as Riesman points out, it also could "... create obstacles to the routine tasks needful in any large enterprise, and [help] to build up fierce suspicions at the least signs of parental bent [i.e., paternalism] on the part of university administrators." It could seriously undercut the symbolic and other roles so important for institutional strength.

Professor Trow's comparisons and contrasts of possibilities for effective leadership in American universities, as opposed to the possibilities in certain European universities, are interesting. Other commentators on the differences, such as Hans Daalder and Edward Shils,[6] have called attention to many of the same phenomena as inhibiting, if not neutralizing, effectiveness in the modern European counterparts. But, I suspect that the differences are not merely interesting in their own historical right: they provide a lesson which can be drawn to illuminate another of Professor Trow's points.

To be sure, the differences do have roots in different conditions of origin, as Professor Trow points out, but it also can be argued that the current difficulty in providing effective leadership in European universities stems importantly from the fact that such leadership was not exercised in Europe during the 1960s and the 1970s. The specific failure can be argued to have been that of blocking claims for equity, for democratization, as the sea change from elite to mass education swept through Europe. The first phase of this change saw junior faculty and students successfully challenge the university governance of fairly autonomous, chair-holding professors. The challenge did not stop there but developed into radical student revolt in several countries, bringing state intervention and the imposition of — as Daalder and Shils say — "centralisation, bureaucratisation, and politicisation" of higher education.[7]

In a word, the current lack of effective leadership in European universities is due, in part, to the fact that effective leadership was not exercised earlier, and not just due to the fact that the origins of European universities were so strikingly different from those of American universities.

The lesson to be learned is drawn out by Roger Geiger, in his review of Daalder's and Shils' work:

> ... any defense of the autonomy of the intellectual functions of the [American] university will have to take into account such realities as the pluralism of American higher education, its responsiveness for good or ill to currents in American society like the civil rights movement, and the irresistible federal presence in supporting university students and university research....
>
> Although bureaucratic aggrandizement may have subsided in the U.S. for the moment, the levers for federal manipulation are now well established.[8]

I think that Geiger's evaluation illuminates the importance of three key points which Professor Trow makes briefly toward the conclusion of his talk; that is, the necessity that the university and its president find a way (1) to serve "... the values both of excellence and of equity," (2) to be seen as doing this, and (3) to do this in such a way that causes these values to be supportive of each other rather than in conflict. This, apparently, the European universities did not, perhaps could not, do. And perhaps, it is becoming more and more difficult for it to be done in America. For instance, Professor Trow talks about the need for equity that spurs Berkeley's responsiveness to minority groups — a need that is becoming ever more pressing in urban centers all over America and certainly in the Southwestern states. At the same time, there is emerging a national clamor for excellence, not only in elementary and secondary education, but in baccalaureate education as well — with five major reports faulting baccalaureate education to have appeared by early 1986.[9] It will be a neat trick for the first-rank universities to both raise standards significantly and ease access significantly in a way that can be seen as moves supportive of each other, rather than moves in conflict. Especially this will be the case if large budget reductions occur in higher education, as some have predicted that they will. If both things can't be done, then we, too, probably can expect greater governmental intervention and greater erosion of institutional autonomy, just as occurred in Europe.

Professor Trow concludes his talk with an expression of confidence in the present and future ability of the American university presidency — especially in the first-rank universities — to exercise effective leadership. The evidence of American educational history seems clearly to justify his optimism. We are indebted to him for his analyses and reflections once again. They should help us better emulate not only the deeds, but the courage, of the great predecessor institutions and their leaders in that history.

References

1. Cohen, Michael and James G. March, *Leadership and Ambiguity,* New York: McGraw-Hill, 1974.
2. Benget, Louis T., Joseph Katz, Francis W. Magnusson, *Style and Substance: Leadership and the College Presidency,* Washington, D.C.: American Council on Education, 1981, p. 4.
3. Veblen, Thornstein, *The Higher Learning in America: A Memorandum on the Conduct of Universities by Business Men,* Stanford, Calif.: Academic Reprints, 1954.
4. Rosenberg, Bernard (ed.), *Thornstein Veblen,* New York: Thomas Y. Crowell, 1963, p. 30.
5. Riesman, David, *Thornstein Veblen,* New York: Charles Scribners, 1953, p. 108.
6. Daalder, Hans and Edward Shils (eds.), *Universities, Politicians, and Bureaucrats,* London: Cambridge University Press, 1982. Chapters 12 (by Shils) and 13 (by Daalder).
7. Ibid., p. 508. Why the European consequences were not the same in America is discussed briefly by Daalder, pp. 508-510.
8. Geiger, Roger, in *The Journal of Higher Education,* 55:3 (May/June, 1984), pp. 415-419.
9. *Wall Street Journal,* "Reports Faulting Higher Education Are Likely to Cause Heated Debate," 19 October 1984.

Response by David A. Whetten

Professor, College of Commerce and Business Administration
University of Illinois at Urbana-Champaign

I appreciate the opportunity to respond to Professor Martin Trow's thoughtful paper. My study of universities-as-organizations has been significantly enhanced by Professor Trow's lucid and insightful writings, and this lecture is certainly exemplary.

It has been determined that only sixty-six institutions in the Western world have survived in recognizable form since 1530. These include the parliaments of the Isle of Man and Iceland, the Roman Catholic and Lutheran churches, and sixty-two universities. From this bit of academic trivia, it is appropriate that the focus of this forum is not whether major research universities can survive their contemporary, but in historical terms rather modest, crises of two percent budget cuts below the rate of inflation salary increases, or modest declines in enrollments, but, instead, whether the leaders at the helm of these durable institutions can alter the course dictated by organizational inertia.

This David Dodds Henry Lecture is a rebuttal of sorts to the talk given to this same forum two years ago by Jim March, in which he proposed his "light bulb theory" of university leadership. He argued that just as we need a light bulb to illuminate our activities in dark rooms, universities need leaders to perform certain obligatory, and largely symbolic, functions. Consequently, he argued further, just as there is little difference between the output of different light bulbs, there is little difference between the impact of different university presidents. Collectively, they perform a necessary function, but individually their actions have little lasting consequence. In response, Professor Trow today has provided a cogent argument for the strong leader view: what makes a difference in shaping organizational outcomes is strong management, not institutional momentum.

While there are obviously many aspects of this fine presentation that I could respond to, I will focus my remarks on what I view as the two major contributions to our understanding of the university presidency.

First, Professor Trow has significantly elevated the debate over the relative strength of the office of the presidency. The typical weak-leader arguments have been based on two lines of thought. Proponents have either concluded, on the basis of statistical evidence, that "on the average, across the entire population of presidents, it does not appear they are having major impacts on their institutions." Or, they have argued logically: (a) there are certain conditions necessary for leaders to be powerful, (b) these do not exist in most universities and colleges; therefore, (c) it follows that university presidents can't be powerful.

In contrast, the typical strong-leader argument has tended to reflect a "cult of the personality" orientation in which proponents cite specific examples where dynamic, smart, or clever presidents have had a significant impact on their schools, and then posit that all leaders with similar characteristics can be equally successful.

Professor Trow has provided a much more solid case for his claim that the university president's role is not inherently weak. He has presented an impressive array of comparative and historical evidence indicating that in this country there has been a trend towards an accrual of power in the president's office. What is particularly noteworthy about his approach is that his argument is grounded in an analysis of structural and contextual conditions, rather than the typical wish list of attractive leadership traits.

While I feel that his arguments, overall, have considerable merit, I have two concerns that will hopefully prompt further examination and discussion of this important subject.

First, I am disappointed at Professor Trow's decision to limit his focus to the major research universities in our country. There are roughly 165 universities classified as Major Doctorals, out of a total population of roughly 3,300 colleges and universities, or about five percent. Consequently, while his arguments in favor of the strong-leader viewpoint are highly persuasive, given his limited focus, it is not possible to reject the statistical argument used by the advocates of the weak presidency. Indeed, implied in Professor Trow's line of reasoning is the conclusion that, except for a relatively small number of "major-doc" institutions, university presidents, in general, are not very powerful.

Second, Professor Trow also hedges his argument by focusing on the potential for power inherent in the office of the president. What is missing is an in-depth analysis of the personal and institutional factors that account for the differences in the abilities of individual presidents to convert the potential for power vested in their office into active personal influence for accomplishing specific objectives.

This limitation actually suggests the second major potential contribution of the paper. Professor Trow does a particularly effective job of highlighting the complexity of the role of university president. Specifically, he argues that there are at least three[*] components of that position: a symbolic role, a managerial role, and an academic or intellectual role. If we add to this a fourth component, the political role, then I would suggest that further analysis of these facets of the president's position may hold valuable clues to how effective presidents are able to transform their potential power into real influence. Specifically, I would suggest that a key to effective university leadership is an academic administrator's ability to: (1) skillfully execute each of these four roles, (2) recognize the interplay between the roles, and (3) decide when it is important to emphasize each role.

For example, my research on effective administrative responses to retrenchment in universities indicates that administrators who respond primarily from a managerial perspective by treating the problem as a budgetary shortfall requiring internal cost cutting measures, and ignore the symbolic, political, and intellectual consequences of this approach, are seldom successful in balancing their budget. Furthermore, they dissipate the potential for using the power of their office to capitalize on an organizational crisis to initiate long overdue changes in the university, for which they have not been able to generate support during periods of prosperity and tranquility.

In these investigations, I was particularly struck by the fact that influential presidents are skillful implementers of the political role, particularly in their ability to mold and manage coalitions of interests. These leaders view their universities more like European parliaments than monolithic American hierarchies. Hence, they were constantly cognizant of the need to nurture the support of key constituents — taking the support of no group for granted. To accomplish this, they use a catalytic leadership style. Many authors have extolled the virtues of charismatic leaders who use their attractive personality attributes to gain the support of the group for the leader's vision of the future. In contrast, catalytic leaders work with the group, or representatives of groups, to articulate, tease out, mold, and solidify a common vision. My research suggests that both of these approaches are appropriate in different circumstances, and part of the key to being an influential president is knowing when to use each approach.

Before concluding, I would like to make a general comment about the strong-versus-weak-leader debate in the university governance liter-

---

[*] Later revised to four components, including the political role, in Professor Trow's published paper.

ature. While this debate has attracted considerable attention to the role of the president, as with most polemics, both sides probably reflect a part of the truth. This conclusion has emerged from my interviews with numerous faculty and administrators from a variety of colleges and universities, during which I was repeatedly struck by the deep-seated and broadly held ambivalence regarding the proper role of administrators in the academic governance process. Furthermore, this ambivalence was especially pronounced when the subject was powerful administrators. One example of this ambivalence is the preference expressed by many for a leader who is a strong external advocate of the department, college, or university, but who is simultaneously a weak internal administrator that does not represent a threat to entrenched, vested interests.

This observation suggests that rather than continuing to search for evidence to support either the strong- or weak-leader theories of the university presidency, a more fruitful line of inquiry for scholars might be to investigate the root causes, manifestations, and consequences of this ambivalence regarding powerful leaders within the academy.

In conclusion, then, this lecture has added considerably to our understanding of the role of the president of contemporary American research universities. The author's extensive and expansive study of this subject is obviously apparent in his presentation. He has been most helpful in providing a historical and comparative background for understanding a very complex, and often oversimplified, debate in this area.

Questions and Discussion

Chancellor Everhart: I have asked Professor Trow to respond briefly to the remarks made by our three panelists, and then I'll open the session for questions from the audience. I hope we can have a fairly general discussion of this important topic.

Professor Trow: I wish to acknowledge with great thanks the care with which members of the panel listened or read, and the courtesy and insight that they brought to bear in their remarks. I could, of course, say quite a lot. Let me just make one remark about each of the panelists' responses.

President Ikenberry was very kind and didn't give me much room to disagree, but he did make a point worth making that I didn't, and that is the extent to which people have excessive expectations of the president. I kept emphasizing the president's genuine powers, but in the minds of some, they are unlimited. There is on one side the assertion that the president has no power at all, it's all fanciful, and so forth; on the other, there is a mythological superman who can leap over tall buildings. The president has both to know the limits of his own power and to be able effectively to educate his constituents to the real limits of that power. If he overstates the case, then he essentially undermines his capacity to do anything. The president has to be the best educator on campus, to teach the various changing constituencies what they can reasonably expect of him. What can be expected is neither everything nor nothing, but has to be continuously explored and restated, as much in action as in words, during his tenure.

Joe Burnett said many things I could respond to, but he also stressed the close link between history and organization. In a very interesting remark, he observed that the failure of leadership in Europe currently is related to the weakness of that leadership and its failure in 1968. That is certainly true, but the weakness of leadership in 1968 can be related to many things, among them the organization of the professoriate in European universities and the tremendous power, at least until recently, of the full professor, the *ordinarius*. In most European countries, there is a small number of full professors and a large number of "junior" staff, many of whom are not junior in age nor anything else, except in not having the rank of professor. By contrast, in this country, any and every faculty member who gains tenure can ordinarily expect to become a full professor. This is enormously important in helping us avoid what is in the European university a kind of class struggle, the struggle of the professoriat — that top 5, 10, or 15 percent of the teaching staff — and all the others, that has destroyed the capacity of the European academic profession to act with any common conception of or devotion to their institutions.

Dave Whetten also made a number of important points. I fully accept his addition of the political role, along with the other three, and, indeed, it may be that it is the king of the roles and should be included as a central aspect of the university presidency. I do accept that he is sorry that I limited my analysis to research universities; I had some remarks about why I did that, but cut them out as mere scaffolding. The fact is that to do this analysis properly one would need to develop a typology of institutions of higher education, in the various cells of which the possibilities for leadership are really quite different and, moreover, don't change in a linear way from the academically most distinguished to those which do not do much research or academic work. For example, the survivors of the nineteenth century college are the small denominational colleges and the historically Black colleges, and there the president is still the enormously powerful czar that he was in most American colleges before the Civil War. Similarly, in some, but not all, community colleges, the president has a possibility for action and initiative by virtue of local support and connections with many local constituencies that the president of the modest four-year state college down the road, governed from the state capital on a line-item budget, does not have. So we have to differentiate this system in a way that really wasn't possible here, in order to develop this kind of analysis at all well for the whole range of 3,200 institutions.

Questioner (William Prokasy, Dean, Liberal Arts and Sciences, University of Illinois at Urbana-Champaign): I would like to ask a question about the particular form that the leadership for the presidency takes on the issue of liberal education. Kerr recently pointed out that he felt that the presidency has largely reneged in responsibility in this arena, and I would be curious to know what kinds of power a presidency has, and what you think the role of president can, or ought to be, in liberal education at a research institution — the sixty-six institutions to which you referred.

Professor Trow: Well, I think it was David Saxon who, in his farewell remarks as he left the presidency of the University of California, said some unkind things about the undergraduate programs of the several campuses, to which, equally unkind, I said to somebody, "How does he know?" But I think that President Saxon, in the course of doing his job very well, had not been required to look very closely at what was going on in the undergraduate programs on the several campuses of the university. That would really be a microstudy, and I think that most of what happens in liberal education on a campus happens invisibly. My own sense is that the most interesting and important things that happen in the private life of the university, in the classrooms and labs where teaching and research go on, are not very visible, nor are they publicized, and often are not known in very great detail to the chief campus officer or to the president.

I think that the chief campus officer has real responsibilities to liberal education, to continue to support it and to make resources available to it, so the people who actually are doing it are not terribly constricted and always at bay. For example, to tax the overhead money that comes in with research grants, largely from science and technology, to tax that money for the support of the humanities is a right and proper function of administrative leadership. To reallocate funds in that way, to try to maintain a balance of subjects and between teaching and research, to resist the enormously volatile movements of student sentiment between one department and another, or between the professional schools and the arts and science departments, those are important functions of the president. I think that I would leave the shaping and content of undergraduate education to the people who are directly involved with it: the academic offices, the chairmen, and the people who actually are doing the teaching and scholarship.

Questioner (Professor Whetten): I was particularly interested in your comments concerning excellence and equity and that marvelous tension which exists between the two, and the president's role in dealing with that tension. My question is this, "Does the president simply work for these two when tension exists, or should the president do something to maintain that tension?" Another way of putting it, perhaps is, "When there is more rhetoric than tension, what does the president do?"

Professor Trow: Well, in the part of the world where I live, there is quite a lot of tension between concepts of equity and excellence. The president doesn't have to encourage it. And I think that is true in many parts of the country. The pressures on presidents to respond to a variety of concerns in the larger society, both moral and political, are very strong — especially in public universities. I gave an example of an area in which these tensions could be resolved by a form of institutional insulation; the actors in two different programs were not particularly aware of what was going on in the other. But in this case, if they had been aware, they wouldn't have been disturbed by it. That is to say, the work in the university in local secondary schools is not in any serious way incompatible with the work that the biologists are doing in molecular biology, nor is the reorganization of biology at all troublesome to the people working in Oakland high schools. As I said in my prepared remarks, efforts to strengthen local central city high schools are in the service *both* of equity and of excellence. But that is not always the case.

In the area of faculty appointments and the application of affirmative action to faculty appointments, the issues of equity and excellence are very sharp and can't always be neatly resolved by a creative president. There may be a very sharp tension in the appointment of specific people, as between the criterion of competitive excellence and the issue of gender or ethnic group representation on the faculty, trends in that regard, and what the legislature thinks about that. There is no easy resolution for those tensions, not in the happy way that I could describe in the example that I gave, and if I have any apologies to make, it is that I chose an example here that is relatively easily resolved. But if presidents don't solve those, they don't get to solve the others either.

Questioner: How important in the educational preparation of a president is a thorough grounding in educational sociology?

Professor Trow: I really don't know, except that I tend to think that effectiveness and sophistication, in the sense of being articulate about the job, are unrelated. I happen, for obvious reasons, to like to talk to presidents who are reflective and thoughtful about their jobs, but the president of a very well-known, small liberal arts college was one of the most sophisticated organizational theorists I've ever known and a disastrous president. He almost wrecked his institution, but, by God, he was clever. And I've known some very effective presidents who could never really articulate, or maybe they chose not to, what it was they were doing, but flew by the seat of their pants and had kind of an intuitive sense of how to function. Being able to articulate the purposes and mission of an institution is important for a president, but not being able to analyze how it works, the way sociologists do, is no great handicap.

Questioner: You were introduced as a person who has finished a term as chairman of the academic senate on the Berkeley campus. I think you alluded to the role of faculty versus the role of professional employees versus the role of nonacademics and other groups on campus, students. I think I read you correctly as saying that perhaps while they all have a role to play, the faculty has a separate and distinct role to play and that really shouldn't be confused with other roles. I guess what I would really like to know is whether or not I read you correctly, and then perhaps you will elaborate on your thoughts on faculty governance or the role of faculty governance and how that interacts with the chancellor a bit more.

Professor Trow: That is an enormously big question that you opened up. I don't know if there is a short answer. In most universities, there is something like an academic senate. I think it has an extremely important role, particularly in the defense of academic standards and in strengthening the president's hand in saying "no" to all the pressures that are on him. I think that it's very often extremely helpful for a president to say to somebody outside who wants him to do something or other, "Well, I really would like to do that, but I don't think my faculty would let me." Now, he can't do that very effectively if, in fact, they would let him. They have to not let him sometimes, and the question is how do they not let him, and do they have to have a big and public uprising, do they have to have votes of no confidence? I think quite a lot of the time the senate can set limits on the president's power by a steady statement of what the university is, to remind him what the central functions of the university are, with due recognition on their part that usually he's serving their interests in his ways as well as his in theirs.

I don't believe a senate can be a form of legislature of the university and, therefore, I would not on the whole think it a useful thing for the senate to also include representatives of students and nonacademic staff. I think that those groups have, and ought to have, a voice in the governance of the university directly to the president, and he has to find ways to take their advice and listen to their concerns, as well as the faculty's, and decide what weight to give to what group on what issue. There is, in many places, an effort by students to gain access to the meetings of the academic senate and have their say there because there's a myth that that's where the university really is run. Insofar as that's effective, it simply dilutes the clarity of the faculty's own views. It also destroys the faculty meeting as a place where a faculty can come to discover what its own mind is, so it gets to arguing issues that are on the students' agenda, very often different issues than the faculty want to discuss.

Also, there is a myth that the students who speak at such meetings represent "the students." Well, they often don't represent the students, but a very tiny group of students who are very political and are, in a sense, serving apprenticeship for a future political career. Also, it's important for them, if they are not to become utterly anonymous, to oppose, to find some dramatic position to sustain, and to complain, so quite a lot of the time their positions are driven by personal and political ambitions.

So where students are members of academic senates, the conversation in those meetings get distorted by a lot of considerations that are not really central to the faculty's own affairs — they have enough to worry about besides those things. But I must say there are many different views on this, and I'm not sure that mine are going to prevail. We're discussing this, yet again, at Berkeley. This never goes away. I want to stress, however, that that simply isn't an adequate analysis of university governance; that's just a beginning of such a thing.

Questioner: You spoke quite distinctly about three* kinds of leadership. You talked about symbolic leadership, and then David Whetten came along and added one called political leadership, and you didn't argue with him. Would you make a clearer distinction whether or not you really think those are two? I think a lot of people in education are a bit uncomfortable with using political leadership as a clear description and are probably more comfortable with saying, "This is symbolic leadership." Do you really make distinctions between those two, or would you think there's quite a bit of overlap in your definition?

Professor Trow: I think the political dimension of leadership of a public university involves knowing the map of the legislature and of its relevant committees; knowing something of the nature of the university's political resources in the alumni and in other groups; knowing of when something important to the university is afoot in the state capital; whom to call among his leading alumni, whom to call on his Board, and whom to call in the legislature; and what kinds of people and resources to bring together when something needs to happen. Now, that isn't the same as the ability to articulate and embody the values of the institution. It is the much more homely business of wheeling and dealing, and yet I think that is a dimension of the role of the president that we would neglect to our peril. But I'm happy here to be corrected by the sitting presidents. I suspect that they have to know and do those things, and I don't find that to be an illegitimate business at all. Is that fair?

Questioner (William Staerkel, President, Parkland College): I was talking to one of our legislators recently — the last session of the legislature, in which, incidentally, higher education came off very well — and he commented to me that the reason higher education came off so well in this last session was because of the president's actions. He said he came to the capitol, he talked to legislators, visited them in their offices; they were flattered. He talked to them about the problems of the university, and they were pleased, and he created an attitude within the legislature that caused them to give higher education more this year than they had gotten before, so I think that clearly points out that it is an invisible fourth element of leadership which is more than just some symbolism.

---

* Revised to four, including political, in Professor Trow's published paper.

President Ikenberry: Well, that says it better than I can by a long shot. In order to give Professor Trow a relief, and since it has gotten awfully close to home, maybe I'd better make a comment. I don't have any problem with adding the fourth category, either, so long as it's understood to be a small *p* political. And it is really more, if you listen carefully to what Martin is saying. It is more than the political process itself as embodied in state government. One can underestimate the importance of having rapport with the governor's office and understanding the legislative process and having rapport with legislative leaders. But I think the dimension that is being talked about here, using the word *political*, really goes beyond that to the broad range of constituencies that might be defined as public constituencies — some of whom are on campus, but many of whom are off the campus but have direct and indirect linkages back to the campus. Furthermore, if they aren't understood, you can't understand how universities function and how decisions get made.

Literally there are hundreds and thousands of farmers across this state and there are organizations through which they come together. The relationship between them and our College of Agriculture, the College of Veterinary Medicine, and the relationship to the legislative process on the one hand and our faculties on the other — it is the complexity of that network, and the university understanding where its power base is, and the president nurturing this power base that determines the final result. And the same must be said of the business community, the legal profession, dentists, pharmacy, medicine, and engineering. This is where a public university president must go. Understanding the complexity of these networks, being able to work with them, energize them, lead them, is the key element.

May I just make one other comment in response to a question that was raised earlier in terms of the relationship between quality and access? I think this is a good illustration of the positive power of the presidency if it's creatively used to do two fundamental things. Number one is help define the question. If the question is improperly defined, improper answers and hypotheses will be forthcoming. The genius of American higher education has been the conviction that pursuing quality and broadening access are not antithetical. One of the roles of a president is to teach the public, his own Board of Trustees, and others: "Now, as before, we are going to pursue these objectives of quality and access in tandem." Failure to exercise that leadership role on the part of the chancellor or the president can take an institution down a negative spiral.

Professor Trow: Can I just add one sentence on this? The reason I believe that the present discussion about secondary education may have somewhat more substantial effects on the secondary schools than did the comparable fuss after Sputnik is that then small groups here and elsewhere got together and wrote better secondary curricula. They put them in bottles, and corked them up, and threw them in the ocean — hoping that somebody would find them. There was a general feeling among educational reformers in universities that it would be a good thing if secondary schooling were better, but I don't think on the whole it happened.

Now, universities like this one, and my own, and others around the country recognize that we cannot resolve this issue of excellence and equity unless secondary education is better, and so for the first time since the 1890s, and maybe earlier, the universities and colleges are beginning to take a bigger role — and not just through their Schools of Education, although in part through their Schools of Education — in secondary education. It is not an act of charity, not a basket at Thanksgiving, but an act of absolutely desperate self-preservation. If we are to remain universities of high quality that also broaden our access to higher education, then we have to do something about primary and secondary education, particularly secondary education.

Questioner (Jo Ann Fley, Associate Professor of Higher Education, University of Illinois at Urbana-Champaign): In many ways, this lecture and the discussion afterwards should have come three years ago, because in some ways we are reacting to, or taking a different approach to, the ideas that James March shared with us. I think your ideas are somewhat contrary to his, and I want to believe some of the things you are saying. I would rather not believe the models that he proposes, but I'm particularly interested in the part about a leader having some discretion and through that, some power, and in your discussion of the power of receivership. We have a joke around here that if you want to do away with an academic unit, in an evaluation simply say that it is not as strong as it could be, it needs more resources to be strengthened and that's the kiss of death. If you want to keep it, recommend that it should be abolished, but those kinds of recommendations usually come from committees or lower administrators. Then what usually happens, as far as I can see, is the implementation of the political model. You wait for parents to get aroused, you wait for a woman to get aroused, you wait for pressure groups to come into the picture, and the recommended unit for being abolished is saved through the political process. The political process doesn't take effect too much in the other case of just recommending that something be strengthened. It seems to me that the political model, or the model of ambiguity, explains the dynamics of that better than claiming that somebody at the top is exercising rational leadership. Does that make sense? Would you care to talk more about the dynamics of this and defend your point of view?

Professor Trow: Well, the issue of taking a school or department "into receivership" caught my attention, partly because it's both obvious and unnoticed. We all know it is done, but nobody seems to have talked about it very much. The surprising thing is that when it happens, there is remarkably little resistance or opposition within the faculty — probably because it happens rarely enough and in extreme cases, so that there is a general consensus that something really has gone wrong. That is to say, it can be treated as an exceptional case, and the treatment of that case is not going to be an attack on the ordinary processes of academic governance in which the faculty plays a major role. Something has gone wrong, and the president or his senior advisers intervene to help put it right, so that the action is in the service of the fundamental values of the faculty anyway. It ordinarily is not done under the pressure of economic constraint; it's done because something about a department or school has gone sufficiently awry so that its reputation is clearly, visibly declining, people in it are hurting, students are hurting, the faculty is hurting.

In the case of biology in my own university, there were several important departments that almost fell off the bottom of the scale in the last national ratings of graduate departments by the National Academy of Science, and there are some others that didn't do so well. When that happens, the intervention is to try to put things right; a unit or group of units is put into receivership for a temporary period, and it is assumed that it will be put back in the hands of its members as soon as possible. When this happens, with very, very few exceptions, there isn't much of a fuss by the academic community. They know that the people in it cannot do anything to help it, and people immediately around it can't because they will be seen as interfering or taking sides in a terrible conflict. It's precisely the "outsideness" of the president or his provost or senior dean that makes it possible for him to intervene. No, it doesn't happen very often, but it is extremely important that it can, and there are times when departments know "we can't let things go on like this or they will come and take us over." Departments don't like to be taken over, so I think it is more important as a potential than as an actual intervention.

Questioner: I would like to respond to that in the aspect of the specific example or specific problem you cited. One of the failures in the academic enterprise is the failure to recognize that many of the academic decisions that we make have political ramifications. Those who are involved in the decision-making process on the academic side are oblivious to the political ramifications, while on the other hand those who might be sensitive to the political ramifications are oblivious to what's happening in terms of the academic decision. I thought — as you were talking about this marvelous cable that you described earlier, with these strands going through it — that there are these impulses going through the wires, but the wires are insulated from each other and there is no communication early enough in the process. There are very few things that the academic entity cannot do if it does them creatively and wisely and sensitively. Where we run into problems, by declaring we are going to close something, only to find out that's absolutely the last program in the university that will ever close, is where we are so clumsy. You see, we don't recognize that the legislature, the public-at-large are going to have a say in what it is that we do or don't do, and we are going to have to lay some groundwork to explain to them why such and such an action is going to have to take place, before they read it in the newspaper, in order to make the decision stick. So part of it, I think, is simply building bridges within the university community to understand that decisions need to be made upon the merits, but that does not exclude them from external impact or review.

Chancellor Everhart: I would like to make a brief comment, first, Martin, if I may. I would just like to recount an example of academic leadership on a different campus, but one that Professor Trow will know well. At Berkeley in the 70s, the state government was cutting back very strongly. In fact, programs were cut, and I believe one year the Berkeley campus lost 110 positions, which is a sizeable number of faculty positions to lose in one year. The erosion stopped the year the chancellor looked at all the cuts that were proposed in the diminished budget and said, "We can't take any more out of academic programs," and he proceeded to take all the cuts out of the administrative staff in the chancellor's office. That got the attention of the state legislature; they really knew they were getting down to bone when the chancellor cut his own staff. From then on, I think, there was a healthy respect. This action also gained the support of the Berkeley faculty, as you might imagine, because they had realized all along that the chancellor's office had too much fat — that's always known on every campus — so in one fell swoop, the chancellor took an action that made a difference in the political sense to the legislature and, also, in the symbolic sense to the campus.

Questioner (Bernard Karsh, Professor of Sociology, University of Illinois at Urbana-Champaign): It seems to me that the issue of excellence and equity — I was about to say excellence versus equity, but I'll pose it for the moment as excellence and equity — is likely to be the central issue which will test the competence, the definitions, and the presumptions about the functions of the president of a university in the near term and probably for the long term. The test is largely on the various roles of the president, most importantly the distinction between the role of the president as academic leader and the role of the president as a political leader. In my view, they are not aspects of the same role; they are distinctively different roles, and they call for distinctively different kinds of behaviors and distinctively different kinds of symbolisms.

President Ikenberry: Well, I welcome the comment. If anything I said lent the impression that I thought the tension was going to go away, I certainly misspoke. The tension between quality and equity, quality and access, is as old as universities themselves, and I see it as a continuing, as an endemic, tension. It is a tension that is within not just the University of Illinois, but it is a tension very much alive in society as a whole. The argument I was trying to make is that it is useful for the president to take the position that in order to pursue quality, you don't have to reject the pursuit of equity and access; in order to advance the cause of access in the equity and equality of opportunity, it need not be done at the sacrifice of quality. It is healthy to maintain the tension and to pursue both ideals. If one could have a measure of quality and equity at the University of Illinois in 1953 when you arrived, in 1955 when David Henry arrived, and today, in 1984, my impression would be that we have gained significantly on both points, that we are as strong academically, overall, today and within specific areas, as we were in 1955, and there is a broad range of opportunity available within this institution, perhaps broader today than in 1955.

Professor Trow: First, to support some of these thoughts: British universities, on the whole, don't worry about access, and so when they get into trouble, they don't have any constituencies outside of government to help them. Also, equity and excellence isn't a problem, it's a dilemma; we learn to live with it rather than solve it. But there is something more substantial to say, and in a way a professor can say it and a president can't. The elected Superintendent of Schools in California, who was defeated the last time — Wilson Riles, a Black man — was, while in office, a member *ex officio* of the Board of Regents of the University of California. When some proposals were made to lower the university's entry requirements, nominally to help the access of minority groups, he voted against it. He said, "Don't wreck the university just now that we are beginning to get into it." I think that the Black population, like other ethnic groups, is not as undifferentiated as it may appear. It is increasingly highly differentiated, and I think we have to learn to talk about ethnic groups with some degree of candor, and not always as they or their spokesmen define the situation or present themselves. Most ethnic group leaders, for obvious reasons and not inglorious ones, assert unity and identity of interest within the group for political strength. But below the surface those groups begin to be highly differentiated, that is to say, more like the rest of us. And it is precisely there that we have to begin to deal with those groups as we deal with all other groups in the society — in some cases finding that they will be a tremendous support for the maintenance of standards in the university, if it is also accompanied by a continued sensitivity to historical injustices that we have inherited.

I think it also does challenge the integrity of a president to talk to different groups, emphasizing this or that and the other thing to each, but fundamentally standing always for the same thing and not for really different things, because if he stands for different things to different groups, he will over time forget who he is in front of what group, and that is a hopeless position. So, after all the analysis of organization and environment, of staff and politics and symbolism, the last word on university leadership must be the absolute importance of a president's personal integrity. And that is surely a fitting note on which to end a lecture and discussion in honor of David Henry.

John Brooks Slaughter, president of Occidental College, has distinguished himself as a student, educator, public servant, scientist and engineer. Throughout his career, he has been active in national efforts to involve minorities in science and engineering. He received his bachelor's degree in electrical engineering from Kansas State University in 1956. In 1960, he began a fifteen-year association with the Naval Electronics Laboratory Center where he became head of the Information Systems Technology Department. During these years he also completed an M.S. in engineering at U.C.L.A. and Ph.D. in engineering science at the University of California at San Diego.

Dr. Slaughter was director of the National Science Foundation and chancellor of the University of Maryland (1982-1988) before going to Occidental. His public service includes the presidency of the San Diego Urban League and vice chairman of the board of directors of the San Diego Transit Corp. His dedication to minority education is evidenced by his service to the Institute of Electrical and Electronic Engineers Minority Committee and the National Academy of Engineering Committee on Minorities in Engineering. Dr. Slaughter has received more than 15 honorary degrees, including one from the University of Illinois.

The tenth Henry Lecture was presented October 17, 1985, at the University of Illinois at Chicago.

Innovation and Tradition in Higher Education

by John B. Slaughter
Chancellor
University of Maryland

I am deeply honored to have been invited to offer you my thoughts today in this very distinguished lecture series. It is a special pleasure to visit the University of Illinois at Chicago because of my great friendship with and great respect for your chancellor, Don Langenberg. Today I want to talk about some of the challenges before higher education — challenges that require, on the one hand, a reassertion of traditional educational values and, on the other hand, innovative approaches to special opportunities.

Within the past year we have seen a spate of major studies on higher education, particularly undergraduate education. Reports from the National Institute of Education, the National Endowment for the Humanities, the Association of American Colleges, and, most recently, from the Carnegie Foundation paint gloomy pictures of what universities and colleges across the country are offering undergraduates.

We find ourselves taking stock of our educational mission and our responsibilities at the same time that we continue to face enrollment pressures, the proliferation of educational opportunities outside of traditional educational institutions, tighter state and federal budgets, and, in the public educational sector, an increasing number of regulations that whittle away at institutional autonomy.

While it's true that we face both dilemmas and uncertainties, the situation in higher education is neither as dire nor as critical as some have characterized it. I am concerned that in dealing with our problems we become too reactive and cautious and thus fail to take advantage of new directions. I agree with my friend, Father Ted Hesburgh of Notre Dame, when he says that "there is no compelling reason for either panic or euphoria, that what is most certain for the next seventeen years is uncertainty." But I would hope that he is wrong in his assessment "that the expansionist era of 'full steam ahead' through clear seas to wide open horizons is now to be followed by two decades of avoiding shipwreck."

We do not want to lose our ability to marvel at the wonderful potential our institutions have as we navigate difficult waters. "Avoiding shipwreck" suggests a caution that will, at best, keep us from losing ground. It will not permit us to grow. I am reminded of the words of Oliver Wendell Holmes who said: "I find the great thing in this world is not so much where we stand, as in what direction we are moving. To reach the port of heaven, we must sail sometimes with the wind and sometimes against it, but we must sail and not drift, nor lie at anchor."

In order to navigate difficult waters and at the same time not become overly cautious, we need to consider the nature of our institutions. What is this thing we call a university? What are the characteristics that it possesses that make it so important and so highly desired by communities like Chicago and Baltimore and states like Illinois and Maryland? Let me give you one definition that underlies much of what I have to say to you today.

Universities are special places — places where intellectual curiosity and the spirit of inquiry hold forth. Universities are places of edification rather than ossification, places of clarification rather than stultification. They are places where the mind and soul are challenged with new and fresh concepts and theories waiting to be tested and applied. They are intoxicating places in which men and women of rich and diverse backgrounds challenge traditions, precedents, and past practices to explore a new and exciting realm of opportunities. They are places where the arts, the humanities, the sciences, and the professions come together in a synergistic environment which produces progress toward the development of a better world.

Traditional liberal arts education

Recent studies of higher education have been particularly critical of the decline in the traditional liberal arts core. The push toward specialization and vocationalism jeopardizes what we have historically valued in the undergraduate experience. Our high-technology society has become an excuse for abandoning requirements that are essential to our students' intellectual and social growth.

This intellectual and social growth in our students is critically important for the future of our society. Frank Newman makes this point eloquently in his Carnegie Foundation report when he says: "The most critical demand is to restore to higher education its original purpose of preparing graduates for a life of involved, committed citizenship. It is a need which arises from the unfolding array of societal issues of enormous complexity and seriousness." Newman found that students graduating today are less civic-minded and less prepared to assume the responsibilities incumbent on a well-educated citizenry than graduates of just fifteen years ago.

No discourse on priorities in higher education in the future can be considered complete, in my opinion, until we deal with this issue. It is more important, perhaps, than many of those topics that occupy much of our concern today — industry/university cooperative research, new instrumentation in our laboratories, and computers in our classrooms. At some point, educators must come to grips with the need for students to have a greater appreciation for both Milton and molecules, Carlyle and chemistry, Marx and microcomputers, Picasso and picofarads.

We must educate our students to understand the insight of the great black scientist Percy Lavon Julian when he said of the sciences and the humanities, ". . . the goal of both is to enrich and ennoble the good life of man." And this education must come in an academic environment that encourages the exchange of ideas and not just the dissemination of information.

As Father Timothy Healy once observed, "The humanities may not be the engine that drives the ship forward." They may not be a warship's biggest gun or a clipper's most stately mast. But the humanities are our compass and our rudder. They are the gauge we use to find out where we are going. And, ultimately, they are what guide us through the seas of time and circumstance.

Let me draw an example from my own field of engineering. As our knowledge of science and technology expands almost without bounds, the five years of undergraduate education required of most engineers must include more, not less, mathematics, physics, chemistry, and metallurgy. But the expanding set of social, economic, and cultural interrelationships associated with our rush toward high technology calls for a much deeper and more professional understanding of these issues as limitations that are present in his or her designs, theories, and products. Education must come to address this reality.

Roger G. Smith, chairman of the board of General Motors, spoke of the importance of these considerations when he said that business is not so much the movement of products as it is the relationship between human beings. That view was echoed by Charles L. Brown, chairman of the board of AT&T, who said: "My own experience has shown that it is the conceptual issues and problems in business — the humanistic concerns, if you will — that are the most difficult to deal with and the most crucial to resolve. And so there is a place — a central place — for the humanities and the liberal arts graduate in business. That's the good news. The bad news is that the good news is not better known."

Beyond the needs of the marketplace, we know that an education that stresses the ability to think, to evaluate, to understand ethical and social issues is absolutely essential in this complex world we live in. It is not enough to bang the drum for a liberal arts education because it will make our students better engineers or better business people. We have a moral imperative to nurture in our students a sense of their civic responsibilities. Twenty years ago Martin Luther King eloquently described this need for balance when he cautioned: "Our scientific power has outrun our spiritual power. We have guided missiles and misguided men ... our hope for creative living lies in our ability to reestablish the spiritual ends of our lives in personal character and social justice." In order for the enormous advances in knowledge that we will see during this decade and in the coming ones to be used for the betterment of humankind, we must have experts who understand the social and philosophical consequences of their work.

In this era of highly specialized training, we must remind ourselves of the purpose of universities. IBM can offer continuing education in the workplace, but major corporations cannot bring together the philosopher, the physicist, the historian, and the microbiologist to offer our students and our society an understanding of the critical connections among disciplines. It is one thing for a microbiologist to understand and master the complexities involved in genetic engineering; it is quite another thing for that future researcher or teacher to grasp the profound moral implications of genetic research.

Striking a balance

In order to make these connections for our students, we must all become more invested in our educational responsibilities. Virtually every major university has a mission statement that includes research, teaching, and service. Nevertheless, at research universities, we tend to emphasize our special interests to the detriment of our common educational goals. For too long, I believe, graduate schools have held themselves aloof from educational responsibilities. They have seen themselves as research centers, as "think tanks," and as vocational training grounds for various professions. To be a member of the graduate faculty at most institutions means you teach less and do more research. You are a member of the faculty elite, and you no longer bear responsibility for the undergraduate program. Just as it has been fashionable over the last ten years for college and university faculty to bemoan the poor quality of high school education, so, too, it is acceptable for graduate faculty to grouse about the quality of students with baccalaureates.

A few years ago, Peter Drucker pointed out the problems inherent in the relative isolation of graduate schools from the educational process. He noted that "where there are great strengths, there are also great limitations." As we all know, our graduate schools produce virtually all of the faculty who teach in all of our colleges and universities. And as the recent reports on undergraduate education remind us, we are not doing a good job of teaching those future educators how to teach and advise. We are not fostering in them a commitment to the educational values that constitute undergraduate excellence, nor are we setting an example for educators at all levels. Universities, especially research universities, must accept some of the responsibility for the current crises in precollege education. We train the teachers; we set the standards; we must be much more aggressive in making the connections. Despite recent initiatives at the state level, we are not offering precollege students enough math and science, nor are we encouraging the balanced programs students need.

Fulfilling the educational mission of turning out civic-minded, well-rounded students is not the exclusive domain of undergraduate institutions and programs. I believe our graduate programs and our research universities must shoulder their share of the responsibility. At the same time, I certainly do not believe that devotion to research is incompatible with our educational mission. As a former colleague of mine used to say: "Research is to teaching as sin is to confession. If you do not participate in the one, then you have nothing to say in the other."

Right now research universities are at a crossroads. In general, the costs of both basic and applied research exceed the universities' capacities to keep pace both in terms of instrumentation and personnel. At the same time, an increasing proportion of federal funding for research and development has been going to defense-related industry.

Research universities have turned increasingly to defense related research and to industry partnerships for support, but these ties create problems that we are just beginning to confront. Universities have a vested interest in academic freedom and the open exchange of ideas. Classified research for the Department of Defense and proposed restrictions on the sharing of "unclassified" information present formidable obstacles to the research and educational agendas of universities. A similar problem obtains with industry's desire to protect its rights to the results of research.

Another problem that is less immediate, but no less significant, is the orientation of these partnerships toward short-term results with immediate applications. It is true that application in many fields is moving closer and closer to fundamental, basic research. I think the boundaries between basic and applied research have achieved a healthy blurring in recent years. Nevertheless, universities must, in most instances, be in the business of nurturing new ideas and making the potential innovations resulting from research apparent — rather than developing the products themselves. Universities must measure partnerships that support research in terms of the common good. We must provide both leadership in setting the research agenda and technical know-how.

At the same time, universities face an important dilemma in making long-term research commitments on the basis of federal funding. In the past thirty-five years, the federal government has become the primary source of all basic research and much applied research support. Federal funding, however, has not been immune to political trends, and it is often difficult to predict the upcoming cycles in funding. Right now, for example, energy research is "out" — not because the national need in this area has abated, but because of a political decision to spend our money elsewhere. We need better long-range planning at the national level for scientific research and better coordination among the many agencies of the federal government that provide support for scientific research. The academic community has a responsibility to monitor federal funding trends and decide whether these trends serve the best interests of the nation.

Changing student populations

Finally, let me address briefly the changing demographics of higher education. If we have not had the dropoffs in enrollment that were predicted for higher education several years ago, it is because we have experienced some changes in our student populations, particularly at public institutions — changes that I believe will strengthen our universities and our society. We have more minorities, more students over the age of twenty-five, more women, more part-time students. While institutions pay lip service to the advantages of these shifts, I know that many faculty members and administrators believe deep down that while we must accommodate these new populations — even find ways to attract them — they do not represent "the best and the brightest." So while warm bodies are welcome, some meet with resistance and, on occasion, hostility as they enter the world of higher education.

I have said many times that excellence and elitism are *not* synonymous. I do not believe that institutions that stress diversity in their student bodies abandon a commitment to excellence. In fact, I believe that the challenge of reaching out in some energetic and affirmative ways to identify, recruit, enroll, and graduate those students who in the remaining years of this century are the ones who will be knocking on higher education's door is one of the great opportunities in higher education today.

We have an opportunity to learn from these students, too. Many have life experiences that motivate them to seek the important interdisciplinary connections. Some are less intent on professional training or even on achieving specific degrees and more interested in learning for enrichment. Some come to us with great abilities but incomplete training. We must bring both flexibility and imagination to the task of developing the potential within a diverse student body.

Even if there were not the practical need to reach out to a wider student audience, higher education must heed the moral imperative to do so. We must set an example for a society that has become, at the very least, complacent if not indifferent. If our national leaders will not move forward toward equality of opportunity, we must provide the direction. I am disturbed by the fact that since 1978 black undergraduate enrollment in colleges has actually declined from 10.8 percent to 8.9 percent in 1982. In 1982, blacks accounted for only 5 percent of the enrollment at major research universities, 9.8 percent at four-year institutions, and 10.3 percent at two-year colleges.

The situation in our graduate schools is especially disturbing. Black enrollment in graduate school has declined from more than 6 percent to 4.2 percent, with Hispanics staying stable at 2.5 percent over the last five years. In 1983, out of a total of 31,190 doctorates awarded, only 1,000 went to blacks and 477 went to Hispanics. By contrast, in 1978, out of 30,850 total doctorates, blacks earned 1,100 and Hispanics earned 532. Blacks and Hispanics are seriously underrepresented in the physical and life sciences, in engineering, and in the professions. Three-quarters of all doctorates earned by blacks are in education and the social sciences. In my own field of engineering, 19 blacks earned Ph.D.s in 1979, and in 1983 the figure rose to 29. I wouldn't say we're on a roll. Finally, 60 percent of all doctoral degrees to blacks in 1980-81 were awarded by 10 percent of the institutions that offer such degrees.

We all know some of the reasons for these sorry figures. The situation arises in part because minorities are not identified, recruited, and encouraged to attend universities and colleges. It arises in part because they are less prepared and more financially dependent. We know that there are not enough blacks in higher education — not enough black administrators, not enough black faculty, not enough black graduate or undergraduate students. Only about 4 percent of all faculty in this country are black, and the majority of those teach in traditionally black colleges. Black administrators make up less than 7 percent of the total.

Finally, we must keep in mind that while over half of our undergraduate students are women and over half of the doctorates awarded in 1983 went to women, women are not well represented on our faculties, especially in the science and engineering fields. We cannot have outstanding graduate programs until every barrier standing in the way of full and equal participation in our academic community has been toppled and replaced with an incentive. We cannot afford to wait fifty years for the underrepresented to become fully represented. We must work aggressively to redress historical injustices and inequities. We must attend to these responsibilities both through our professional commitments and programs and at a personal level, with offers of help, support, and mentoring.

Conclusion

Most of you, I am sure, are familiar with Peters and Waterman's influential book on corporate America, *In Search of Excellence*. Those authors identify eight basic principles to account for the success of our best-run companies. For me, the most compelling of these principles is one that calls for establishing a climate in which there is dedication to the central values of the company combined with tolerance for all employees who accept those values.

Higher education is in the process of taking stock, and we have an important opportunity right now to reassess our values and to offer leadership to all educational levels. To do this, we must think in the terms that Frank Newman outlines, "Policy makers must be willing to examine whether current programs and policies are achieving their educational and scholarly goals, not just whether they are meeting their financial and administrative requirements."

Research universities must find ways to reestablish the traditional ties across disciplines, to ensure that research in all disciplines is informed with a spirit of civic-mindedness and has as its end some contribution to educational excellence and the public good. As the problems we face become more complex, it is sometimes easier to isolate the small components and assume that a scientific, technical, or even literary problem can be studied outside of a larger context. One of the principal reasons for keeping research in the university is to ensure that this isolation does not happen and that we continue to make the connections for ourselves and our students.

The nationally syndicated columnist, William Raspberry, spoke at one of our recent commencements and urged our graduates not only to do well but also to do good. This simple credo is the bedrock of the values I would like to see higher education embrace. As Martin Luther King once noted, "We must use time creatively . . . and forever realize that the time is always ripe for doing right."